A Mother's
Intuition

A Mother's Intuition

Autism—A Journey into Forgiveness and Healing

Catherine Marinelli-Gagliano

As told by: Linda Pedreira

TRUE DIRECTIONS
AN AFFILIATE OF TARCHER BOOKS

iUniverse®

A MOTHER'S INTUITION
AUTISM—A JOURNEY INTO FORGIVENESS AND HEALING

iUniverse books may be ordered through booksellers or by contacting:

iUniverse
1663 Liberty Drive
Bloomington, IN 47403
www.iuniverse.com
1-800-Authors (1-800-288-4677)

Because of the dynamic nature of the Internet, any web addresses or links contained in this book may have changed since publication and may no longer be valid. The views expressed in this work are solely those of the author and do not necessarily reflect the views of the publisher, and the publisher hereby disclaims any responsibility for them.

Any people depicted in stock imagery provided by Thinkstock are models, and such images are being used for illustrative purposes only.
Certain stock imagery © Thinkstock.

ISBN: 978-1-4917-4285-3 (sc)
ISBN: 978-1-4917-4286-0 (hc)
ISBN: 978-1-4917-4284-6 (e)

Library of Congress Control Number: 2014913518

Printed in the United States of America.

iUniverse rev. date: 08/08/2014

*T*his book is dedicated to my friend, teacher, and confidante in heaven: Maureen Polinice, and my sons Anthony and Michael, for they have challenged and inspired me to become the mother and woman I am today.

My husband and father to our sons, Anthony, for believing in me and our family.

My parents and mom-in-law, Armando, Angela and Frances, who are the backbone and foundation of our family. They have taught me the true meaning of faith and determination.

My friend Terry Lauria, who gave me solid advice, compassion, and understanding when times were difficult.

A special thanks to my editor, Linda Pedreira, a one of a kind lady without whom I could not have taken this journey.

Thanks to GOD for making all things possible, showing me that miracles do exist, and confirming the true power of prayer.

My neighbors Richard and Loretta, for whom thanks is just not enough.

Patty I., for always having my back and believing in me... My soul-sister and cousin Donna, who always knows what I need, even when I don't... Patty P. for friendship and understanding... Jeanne and Jenna for always inspiring me...Lynn R. for always supporting me...and Diedre Hallett, for encouraging me to push forward and never letting me forget my inner strength.

Mrs. Pat, Mrs. Mary Jane, Mrs. Josie, Mrs. Linda P., Mrs. Janine F., Mr. Michael W. and Mr. Ivan R. for their patience and support while teaching my children.

Danielle Brooks and Paulette Palmer of the DanLette Agency for their friendship, advocacy, and support of my special needs children.

Coaches LaBella, Hoffman and Weiss for teaching team sportsmanship and setting a good example. Challenger Division Little League for giving Anthony the opportunity he would never have had.

Thanks to Laura Ryan Photography, not only for her patience but her beautiful work.

For those of you I have not mentioned, I sincerely thank you for being the angels on earth that have crossed my path and who have played a special role in raising both my children.

*T*hanks to the entire staff at C.D.D. for being "the village" in raising my son Anthony.

As a parent of a special needs child, I am a lifelong member of a unique club of people with a common bond, that of sharing the joys and challenges of raising children who are specially gifted.

The staff at C.D.D is part of my club too. You have chosen to share your amazing skills, compassion, and gifts with my child. You certainly had the choice to do other things and use your many talents elsewhere.

I am glad you chose to be part of the C.D.D. family, and I am grateful for what each of you gives of yourself every day to make our children's days brighter and more meaningful.

My son is a better person for having known you. You have made a very positive difference in his life -- and in mine!

Thank you for all that you do, and for being part of my club and the C.D.D. family!

Love & light,

Catherine Marinelli-Gagliano

Contents

A Mother's Intuition

Foreword ("Forward")

The book's timeline begins at the present and ends in the past as an attempt to mirror how my life has progressed. In other words, although the life of a parent of a child with special needs may often appear to be topsy-turvy to those on the outside, there is a definite itinerary. Sometimes we take one step forward and three steps back, but we do advance eventually. That is why the book's format is an atypical one. It may be confusing at first, but you will be able to get a handle on it as you proceed to read. By writing it in this way, I am giving you a glimpse into my world.

CHAPTER 1

"Go Chiefs"

The Element of Surprise

*J*n the summer of 2013, my son Michael was going through a definite transformation. I guess you could say that he was really coming into himself. He always appeared to be in deep thought, thinking about the excitement of going to a new middle school, making new friends, and leaving elementary school and his painful past behind. He would openly discuss bullying and question why it was so difficult for children and adults to just accept the differences that exist in everyone. There was a time in the recent past when I couldn't have had these discussions with him because it would have hurt us so badly. Just a few years earlier, he was being tormented to such a point that he was experiencing night terrors, anxiety and an absolute loathing of school.

Wow! How time flies… Michael was now entering middle school and looking forward to playing football. He had taken a break from the sport due to the incessant teasing and harassment that had been going on at that time. Whenever he attached himself to a few of his teammates, he had to endure the most brutal insults, which was why I was proud, yet fearful when he said he was going to give football another try. I could not help but remember how Michael had been misdiagnosed with ADHD, a mistake both of us had had to live with because the prescribed remedy did not address his panic attacks both on and off the playing field.

It was a beautiful day in September; I was picking Michael up from football practice. Football practice occurred every single day after school for two hours. I could see from the distress in his face that something had happened. During practice, one of the bigger players had threatened to throw an entire cooler of water at him.

Michael had warned him, "Don't even think about it. If you do, you will regret it!"

The other boy threw the water and the cooler anyway. In response, Michael ran towards him, grabbed him by his front shoulder pads, threw him to the ground, and pushed his helmet into the dirt.

I was flabbergasted. Michael had once pointed this same player out to me. This kid was as big as a giant even without his equipment!

When I finally found my voice, I told him I was pleased he had defended himself.

However, Michael did not want to discuss the incident further: "Please don't be proud of what I did because I don't like treating anyone like that. I only did it because I had no choice." Apparently my son, the boy who had been the long-suffering target of dozens of such bullies so many years ago, no longer existed. His coach assured me that Michael had handled himself very well. The following day, the coach informed me that the bully was going to run laps all during practice as punishment. I was elated that someone was finally being held responsible for their behavior.

It is very unfortunate that we still need to teach our children about the cruelty that continues to exist in the 21st century. As parents, we find ourselves forced to show our children how to protect and defend themselves, even if it makes them uncomfortable to sink to that level of behavior. We need to remember that children are a product of their environment; we all know that *the apple doesn't fall far from the tree*. As adults, we should first examine ourselves to make sure these behaviors are not being taught at home, whether consciously or unconsciously. Second, we should recognize that our children are not perfect angels and are capable of doing anything when not in our company. Third and most importantly, we must learn and then teach our children to accept what is different in our society and not to judge others.

CHAPTER 2

"Take Me Out To the Ball Game"

Anthony, Jr. Is Playing Baseball

*J*t was March 2013: My older son Anthony's behavior specialist and mentor called to tell me that a local baseball league had a division for special needs children. Anthony, Jr. had always been passionate about baseball and his dream was finally about to come true. He would be in the Challenger Division Little League. My heart was dancing for him. Finally he would get to experience what he loved most - with children who would accept him - and with coaches that had hearts of gold and saintly patience.

Anthony's first game was played in the second week in April. I made sure Grandma Angela marked it on her calendar so that we could go and support him on opening day. She was so excited for him that she began to cry. When that day came, my parents met us at the field.

The Challengers play ball unlike most Little League teams. There's no such thing as a strike or a ball since every player can stay at bat until they get a hit; they don't even keep score. However, when you see those players (most of whom have special needs) running around the bases on a beautiful Sunday morning, there's no doubt about it: score or no score, strikes or no strikes, they're having some good old-fashioned baseball fun.

Since its launch in 1998, the Little League Challengers have always been a non-competitive, co-ed league. While the players do get the opportunity to work on their batting and fielding skills, the emphasis is placed more upon providing the benefits of the team sports experience to those who have traditionally been denied it. The true goal is to bring special needs children out on the field to interact with other kids, to breathe some fresh air, and to have a real blast.

That first game in April, I remember it being quite chilly, but not cold enough to frost the warmth in our hearts. As we watched those children giving it their all and being part of a team with their friends, we saw their smiles and felt their excitement. I cannot put my emotions into words...you had to have been there with me all the way to understand how much this game meant to me. Anthony's hero was and still is Derek Jeter, the New York Yankees captain and shortstop for 18 years and 5-time world champion. This he knew about...and now there he was, having his own "Jeter Moment!"

Anthony, Jr. has some arm. He can really hit that ball into another dimension. It's so amazing to watch that you almost forget his disabilities. When I looked at him in his uniform that day, my spirits soared to see him so happy. When he hit the ball, it went over the fence into the parking lot. It was gone! I was wildly screaming at him to run the bases. He made it all the way to home plate! My son, my son, my son! How I love that boy!

For those of you who are fortunate enough to have a child participate in a sport, please understand that while winning is important, it isn't everything. If your child is trying his best, then that's what should matter. You should be elated that they are capable of understanding the game, following the rules, running on two legs, coordinating their bodies, and seeing, hearing, communicating, and doing all the things that parents of healthy children take for granted every day. Recognize that you received the gift of health through your children. Rejoice in your good fortune and don't ever take it for granted.

CHAPTER 3

"Out of the Mouths of Babes"

Hurricane Sandy

*T*hursday, October 22nd, 2012 felt a little different from any other day. I had this queasy, anxious feeling in the pit of my stomach that told me something was going to happen over which I would have absolutely no control. Over the years, we have had a multitude of dire forecasts of storms that somehow just missed Long Island, but now my intuition was telling me that this time was going to be quite different, and yes, as you all know, it certainly was.

The day was a routine one, yet strangely quiet. After I had completed my usual chores, the unsettled feelings I had experienced earlier in the day came rushing back over me. I knew it had to be my "second sense," which had been proven right time and time again. In the late afternoon, a weather alert had been issued regarding a super storm named "Sandy," which was making a steady path towards the tri-state area (New Jersey, Connecticut and Long Island). Despite having heard inaccurate weather predictions like this before, my inner voice told me that Sandy was without question going to be "the big one."

I thought it best to keep my concerns to myself. I took some time to pray and asked whatever force that I was feeling to please keep my family safe from harm. These prayers sustained me, lightening the dread I had been experiencing; in its place stood safety and warmth. Now I was able to breathe easier, knowing that whatever was going to happen, my unwavering faith would protect us all.

My youngest son Michael arrived home from school at 3:30. He tossed his backpack on the dining room table, took off his jacket and shoes and, with his warm smile, asked how my day was and if everything was alright. His next question (not a surprise, given his large appetite) concerned snack time. So I made him a sandwich, while he spoke with excited anticipation about the sixth grade Halloween Parade. This was his last year before graduating from elementary school. I kept my worried thoughts buried deeply inside because I feared that things might not work out the way he thought. However, I was determined not to ruin Halloween for him, one of childhood's favorite memories, so I had hidden the costumes, accessories and candy in the basement as I had always done from the time I was a young mother.

That evening, as my husband and I ate dinner, I spoke of my concerns. He reassured me that he would secure the house and not to worry so much because we live one mile from the water. I knew he was trying his best to calm me, but inside I was not sharing his confidence. While tossing and turning, trying to sleep, I was consumed by maternal instincts to pick up my son Anthony Jr. who lived in a residence for special needs children. After all, he was not that far away and I wanted to keep him safe with us until the storm had passed.

Having made my decision, I drove Michael to school in the morning and then called Anthony's residence. I made sure that the medical office would know to give me enough medications until this unpredictable storm would finally end. It was vital that my family remained all together under one roof now.

I arrived at the residence and Anthony worriedly asked why I was picking him up so early on a Friday morning. This was not routine for him. Grandpa Armando and Grandma Angela usually came to get him on Friday afternoons. By this time, I had had enough life experience to know that my son would sense when things were outside of the norm. So I kissed and hugged him and told him I missed him so much that I wanted to spend a little extra time with him. He was OK with that response, but I could still feel his apprehension. Autistic children are quite capable of sensing heightened emotions around them.

We drove straight home; Anthony was extremely quiet. I gave him a snack and he became preoccupied with his iPad. He asked why our family dog Jake did not leave his cage, and was acting as if he were afraid of something. I was once again astounded by how his keen observation of our dog told him that Jake was not himself that day. He looked at me for an explanation. Not wanting to scare him, I just said that Jake might be a little bit more tired than usual.

I then tried to change the subject, but Anthony pursued the topic by asking if I thought Jake knew about the big storm that was coming. I was surprised that he had already become aware of "Super Storm

Sandy." Years before, he would have not been able to communicate his concerns out loud.

I asked him what he knew about the storm and he said with assurance, "It's going to be big, so we should make sure we take safety precautions for inside and outside our home, for the public to stay inside and, if your mayor or police tell you to leave your home, you leave!"

At this point I was more than impressed with how completely Anthony realized the risks we might be facing.

Michael had just finished learning the consequences of bad weather in his sixth grade science class: the measures you needed to take during hazardous storms and how to keep yourself and your family safe. If you know anything about Asperger children, you understand that the syndrome is all about listening and following the rules. So it was no surprise to me when Michael came home from school that day with a list of things we needed to have in the house: flashlights with working batteries, lots of candles, lighters, canned food, a supply of water bottles, and a generator. By the end of the day, we were as prepared as we could be for what was to come. If it had not been so frightening, I would have felt like we were about to embark on a family adventure.

By Friday evening though, the sense of adventure had turned into something more sinister. To ward it off, we watched television and played a few board games. When it was time for bed, the boys went straight to their room. Around 10:00 PM, it started to rain with some ordinary wind. Maybe it would not be that bad. However, in time, the rain had become tumultuous with fierce uncontrollable gusts. The boys were so frightened that they asked to spend the night in our bed. Jake was crying uncontrollably from his crate. He has a very even temperament, but you could actually hear his fear and distress as he whimpered. We let Jake into our bed and now our family was complete.

It was a night of fear, frustration, anxiety and stress. What would tomorrow bring? The worst was yet to come and my husband and

I knew it. We tried to keep ourselves from the windows, but the howling of the wind and force of the torrents was so frightening that our curiosity sometimes got the best of us. We ached to look outside like children, just to see what was going on.

Then, as our sons looked out of our front window, they saw our neighbor's patio furniture fly over his home and land in his front yard. We were trying to take all of this in when the phone rang: It was my neighbor Lynn. I immediately asked if they were alright. She explained that, while passing her front window, she saw our trampoline (which we thought had been secure enough) sail over the fence and that it was now making its way down the block, rolling on its side. My husband threw on his boots and jacket to help her husband hold onto the trampoline. Then our neighbor Paul, the one who had just lost his patio furniture, ran to help us with his tools. Paul made a quick decision to chop the trampoline into pieces before it damaged property or, even worse, hurt someone.

Anthony Jr. looked at me and said, "Mommy, we have no control over what's going on outside - only God does."

I was having the exact same thought, but he said it aloud... *out of the mouths of babes.* No sooner had he made his pronouncement, we lost all power to our home. We had a radio, but could only listen to the news that the water was rising in certain areas of our beloved town.

I became consumed with worry for my brother because he lived on the south shore near the rising waters. I had faith that he was prepared, but this storm seemed to have an uncontrollable vengeance and I had heard about serious flooding in his area. We had sporadic cell phone service throughout the night, which was very frustrating. Afterwards we found out that he protected his home and family like a true warrior, pumping the water out of his basement throughout the stormy night.

The next day was Sunday; Sandy was gone, but much remained to be done. The destruction and emotional upheaval that this storm left behind was enormous. When you were finally able to drive around, it was difficult to take in all that had happened. It was surreal and quite unbelievable. Our home had no real damage, but we felt terribly for the people who had lost everything or who had had damage to their homes. We were so grateful that we were all safe, including all our family members and close friends.

My boys wanted to know how we could help the community and those in need. We shopped and bought much needed supplies for the elementary school and our church. Our donation consisted of twelve bags of everyday supplies, such as toiletries, canned food, water, etc... Michael looked at me and said it really felt good to give and help others. I made sure that my children knew just how close we had come to being in the same situation.

Despite my enormous sense of fear, I had never felt so very close to God's presence. I had learned firsthand that we are not in total command of our lives. As humans, we would like to believe we can control things, but it is God who has full mastery and may have other plans for us. We lost power for an entire week and for the most part, it was nice to be separated from outside technology, playing board games and having conversations via candlelight. We cherished this special time of being a traditional family, of putting things into perspective, and of realizing what was really important to us. Life is too short to have regrets, so live every day as if it were your last. It is my fervent hope that most of us will walk away from this experience with a lesson or two learned because it the hardest of times that molds our character and defines who we truly are.

CHAPTER 4

"Do I Know That Boy?"

Why My Family?

*A*ugust 20, 2012 started off like any other day. Anthony had stayed with us for an extended weekend. (Anthony usually resides with us on weekends. Now age thirteen, Anthony has been out of our home since he was eight years old.) The alarm sounded at 7AM and I could hear the birds softly chirping outside my window.

With the sun shining into my bedroom, warming me inside and out, I said under my breath, "What a beautiful day…"

Quietly taking my steps ever so lightly around my home so as not to awaken my sleeping boys, I tried to get myself ready for whatever the day might bring.

Just as quickly as the sun hides behind a cloud, my mind went on high alert when, on the other side of my bedroom door, I heard a familiar refrain: "Mommy - it's Anthony - I'm hungry!"

Before I could respond, he galloped into the kitchen, seeking out whatever food was readily available, but he was soon distracted by the plaintive yelping of our dog Jake who wanted desperately to be let out of his crate. Anthony nobly released him, but neglected to open the back door, which was crucial for Jake's physical needs.

Instead, Anthony repeated his "I'm-hungry!!!" mantra without stopping. His **O**bsessive **C**ompulsive **D**isorder was now in full gear and it was not even 8AM yet.

I needed to immediately tend to my son due to his prescribed regimen of medications. I carefully handed him his cocktail of meds in a medication cup. I turned aside to prepare sunny-side up eggs, with well- done bacon and home fries. As I turned to hand Anthony his favorite breakfast, he threw the cup of meds at me.

I was now shaking with anger as I knelt on the floor gathering and counting pills, "one, two, three, four, five six, seven, eight," shaking my head, holding my breath, and asking myself, "Why *me*, why *my* family?"

While picking myself up off the floor, I heard him asking me for ketchup for the fifth time. Before I could open the refrigerator to search for the Heinz bottle, he had finished his breakfast, taken his pills from my hands one by one, and had run without warning out the front door. This is a typical day in the life of a family dealing with the toxic combination of autism and raging teenage hormones. His neurologist had warned me that there would be a long string of days like this once puberty had set in. Anthony's complete menu of diagnoses includes: Pervasive Developmental Disorder, Attention Deficit Hyperactivity Disorder, Obsessive Compulsive traits, Oppositional Defiance, Anxiety, Depression and Epilepsy.

Back at home, my neighbors across the way were listening and staring at the commotion taking place. Of course, I wanted to hide under a rock from complete embarrassment, weary of yet another odd episode at our household. Under my breath, I was thinking that I just wanted all of this to go away. I hadn't signed up for this.

My younger son Michael was awakened by my screams, which had been set off by Anthony running into the street throwing rocks at our front glass door as well as the windows.

With his all-too-familiar look of despair, my younger boy asked, "Mom, are you alright?"

We both went outside and began the ritual of calming Anthony down.

In response, he took off his shirt, hurled it at me, and shrieked, "Leave me alone!"

Feeling helpless, I asked him, "What's wrong?"

In the middle of throwing rocks at parked cars, he suddenly stopped, raised his head to look at me and confessed what I already knew about him deep down inside of my soul: "I want to be good. I don't know why I do what I do."

Before I could stop him, Anthony ran around the corner, in front of my neighbors' home. They are more like my guardian angels, if you ask me.

From their front window, I heard a soft voice: "Anthony, please behave. Listen to your Mom. She loves you. You're going to get hurt. We don't want anything to happen to you."

Michael grabbed hold of his brother, as Anthony continued to kick, shove and bite in protest. I was trying frantically to get them both away from the traffic in the street and back into the safety and privacy of home. My hands and body were shaking uncontrollably. *Why do my neighbors always have to know my business?* I was totally mortified and just wanted to hide out for the day. I just wanted this clown show to end.

In the front door hallway was a pool of urine from my dog Jake. Luckily, this was not normal and only happened when he was stressed. As I searched through the house for Jake, I saw his light beige tail sticking out from under my bed. I wondered if there was room for me under there.

As I turned my head, I could see Anthony out of the corner of my eye. He was hitting himself in the head. I clutched his hands, kissed his face, and cried out,

> "Do you have any idea how much I love you? Please stop hurting both of us in this way…I don't want anything to happen to you. Go lie down on your bed, think about what just happened, and the consequences of what you did!"

These words have become my mantra far more often than I care to admit.

It was only 9AM, but it was obvious at this point that I was going to need outside help. So I tearfully called in my support team, my parents, who could hear the frustration and panic in my voice. As always, they immediately understood what needed to be done. Fifteen minutes later the doorbell rang, both to my sorrow and my relief. It was my heroes who had come to whisk Anthony away and give me a much needed break.

I looked out my window as the car drove away, with Michael at my side.

"Why is he like that, Mom? It's really hard when he comes home because I feel responsible for him even though he's older than me."

His questions made me examine my own role as a parent. Why

couldn't I handle the situation as I knew I should, without having to rely on my parents? And the even bigger accusation: Why did I always feel so guilty?

So, resuming my parental responsibility now that Anthony was out of the way, I reminded Michael of his brother's disabilities. As an eleven-year-old with a recent diagnosis of Asperger's Syndrome, Michael was finding it increasingly difficult to comprehend and deal with his own struggles, much less those of his older brother.

Afterwards, I sat at my kitchen table, holding a wet tissue in one hand and a stale cup of coffee in the other. To think I had awakened early to take care of myself, say a few prayers, and have a few minutes of quality time. What was I thinking?

The morning quickly disappeared; it was time to retrieve Anthony for his 2:30PM neurology appointment. As I drove along with the top down on my Mustang, the stagnant coffee started to churn inside of me, twisting my insides into tangles of knots as I relived the morning's events. When I saw him, he was blissfully unaware of what had gone on just a few short hours ago. I thanked God for small miracles.

We arrived at the neurologist's office at 2:15PM for his routine check-up. Bad news: the doctor was running extremely late due to a new patient's appointment. After sitting for at least an hour, Anthony asked to use the restroom. As I began to close my eyes, I realized that he had been in there too long.

I knocked quietly at the door and heard him say, "I need you Mom."

I looked into the toilet and saw a huge pool of blood. He had torn his anal fissure because of difficult bowel movements caused by his medications. In a moment, he was crying in my arms in the restroom, telling me he was so sorry for making me sad and for being the way he was. I cleaned him up and hoped this awful day would not get any worse.

Both my children were now very hungry and frustrated because of the interminable wait. We were seen approximately 45 minutes later, only to receive a refill on prescriptions. The visit was a rushed one without any sense of accomplishment. Why make any child wait this long? Thank God Grandma Angela had given us some leftover food that was in the trunk of my car. There's nothing quite like homemade pizza, fresh oven baked bread, frittata (egg vegetable pie), fried meatballs and some ice tea to wash it down. Who needed a drive-through?

We drove Anthony back to his "other home" and another wave of unbearable sadness washed over me, caused by the guilt of leaving him behind, the sadness of the morning, and the constant heartbreak of a special needs parent. What did he think about at night when he was lying in his bed alone? Did he think we abandoned him?

On the homebound drive I could not help thinking about what his future would have been like if he had been born neuro-typical. *Would he have been playing sports? Would he have had sleepovers? Would he have had a best friend to confide in? Would he have shared that special bond that only brothers have? What could-have- been for me and my family?* Why did I keep torturing myself with these *would-have/could-have/ should-have* scenarios?

It was now evening, I was lying in bed emotionally exhausted and I could not sleep. I tried to pray, but my guilt continued to eat at me.

I kept asking myself, "Who was that boy in the street this morning? Am I really his mother? Was a mistake made somehow? Was I doing everything that I could for him?"

All this was just too overwhelming to carry inside on a daily basis. What made it more impossible to deal with was the combination of his perfectly beautiful angelic face with his unexpected and frightening outbursts of fury. Strangers would never know how this sweet boy was trapped inside a body of disarray and confusion. My final thought was that this awful day really needed to come to an end so that the sun could rise again tomorrow.

CHAPTER 5

"Hello, is Michael Home?"

The Invention

*M*y alarm went off - it was 8:00 AM. I slowly awakened to "What a Wonderful World" by Louis Armstrong. Its melody and lyrics made me appreciate the beauty and hope that a new day always inspired in me.

As I sprang out of bed and placed my feet on the hardwood floor, I noticed that one of my slippers was missing. The only culprit I could think of was Jake, who I was sure had hidden it among his belongings. Sure enough, as I lifted the blanket off his crate, I could see a small patch of my fuzzy black slipper under his beige curly hair as he slept. He was sleeping so peacefully that I decided to leave him be. If having one slipper would be the worst part of my day, I could handle it.

It was the beginning of summer 2012, and what a hot day it promised to be. On the morning news, the weather forecast predicted temperatures in the high 90's, with the possibility of reaching 100 degrees. I decided to spend the day at the town pool. As I prepared the cooler with ice, made sandwiches, packed drinks, found snacks in the cupboard, and stuffed it all, along with the towels and sun block, into the beach bag, it was time for a second cup of coffee.

As I sat in deep thought wondering what Anthony would be doing for the day at his residence, my phone rang. The very professional voice on the other end asked to speak with Michael.

"He's sleeping at the moment. May I ask who is calling?"

"This is Meghan Walters from the Dannison Corporation."

I was now bewildered and curious. "Is there something I can help you with? I'm his mother."

"Yes, I would like to discuss his email and video correspondence regarding his invention that he submitted to our corporation."

Shocked and nearly speechless, I told her that Michael was only eleven years old. Meghan asked that a conference call be arranged at our earliest convenience to discuss his submission, his ideas on design, the chain of prototyping, obtaining a patent, and ultimately marketing the product to corporations. She then informed me that

I would need to represent him because of his age. Wondering if this was some sort of prank, I told her I would call her back.

I reached for my iPad to search for Dannison Corporation, only to find out it was one of the largest patent invention companies in the United States. WHAT? Could this be? As I scratched my head in disbelief, I decided it was time to wake up Michael to find out more about this mysterious phone call.

In a loud singing voice I called, "Michael - rise and shine!"

Groggily, he murmured, "What time is it?"

"It's 10:30 - time for you to wake up!" He gave me his familiar one-eye-open-yawning-sleepy- head look.

With a smirk on my face, I asked "Did you submit a video and email the Dannison Corporation about an invention?"

"Yes, I did. What's for breakfast?"

Michael went into the bathroom, leaving me just as confused as I was when I first received the telephone call. He then sat at the kitchen table and asked me:

"Mom, I thought I heard the phone ring. Who was that? May I have pancakes?"

"The answers to your questions are: Meghan Walters from the Dannison Corporation about your invention, and yes, you may have pancakes. Now I have a question for you - what invention, Michael?"

"I asked you the other day how an idea for a new product could be turned into something that could be sold to the public. You told me the internet usually has companies that could help submit ideas to present to a corporation. So I did my research, introduced myself by email, sent my idea by video, and that's why she's calling. Good old technology, Ma."

Totally taken aback, I told him we needed to call her back to set up a future conference call because of his age. He had apparently taken care of that legality already by informing her in that first email that I would be representing him.

After breakfast, Michael decided he would call her back to discuss the project further. By this time I was on my third cup of coffee, wondering in disbelief if this was really happening and not just one of my more pleasant dreams. My anticipation was getting ahead of me. It had to be the first time I had ever seen Michael eat so slowly. I recall asking myself if he was really eating that slowly or was it that I lacked the patience to wait for him to make this phone call. Then he had the nerve to ask for seconds! I looked at him sternly.

"You need to make that call! Aren't you the least bit curious about all this?"

He laughed, looked me straight in the eye and said, "No, she can wait."

"If you want more pancakes, you will make that phone call now!"

That did the trick! He dialed the number and put it on speaker. We heard that same lovely voice of Meghan Walters, Vice President of New Products of Dannison Corporation:

> "Your invention has been reviewed by our staff; we are interested in your idea and would like to expand it further. Since you are one of the youngest inventors ever to submit an idea, we will be working closely with you and your mother. We will be sending you a copy of the Dannison Corporation Confidentiality Agreement. When you receive the documents by email, please sign them, fax them back to our corporate office, and then we will set up a conference call to discuss the process further on a future date."

After the phone call, he calmly requested yet another serving of pancakes. At that moment, I was still focused on the conference call that just had taken place.

He looked over at me and announced, "Cool...right? What are we doing today?"

"Michael, I thought we would go to the pool since it's going to be a hot day."

As I handed him another helping and he poured syrup over the pancakes, I was acutely aware that the morning's events hadn't fazed him in the least. This was Asperger's Syndrome at its finest.

An hour later we received the confidentiality agreement by email. We reviewed the document together, page after page. With pride and a great big smile, Michael signed his name.

"Mom can you please fax this back for me?"

I asked him if I worked for him now.

"Yes you do.....I'm on my way to becoming an entrepreneur!"

CHAPTER 6

"Miracles Do Happen"

The EEG

*I*t was March 1, 2012 around 6:00AM. I was exhausted from having to keep Anthony, Jr. awake the night before for today's EEG at the hospital. An EEG (electroencephalogram) is a test that measures and records the electrical activity of your brain by using sensors (electrodes) attached to your head. We sleep-deprive him so that he can stay calm and reach sleep mode while in the hospital bed as the technician monitors him. It is a nerve-wracking experience-before, during and afterwards. Before...because it is emotionally, mentally, and physically debilitating for us to stay awake, knowing what was to come the next day. During - because it is so hard to watch your child go through it all, knowing how scary it must seem to him. After - because we have to wait by the phone every day, dreading to hear the results. Yet, we have had to accept this ordeal every six months since Anthony was first diagnosed with epilepsy at the age of three, and have come to accept it as part of our family routine.

Why was I so tired? Well, my husband can sleep through just about anything, which left me flying solo during the torturous process of sleep-depriving our son. During the night I found myself asking, "Who is really being tortured here – Anthony or me?" He thought of it as one big party with no set bedtime. Despite my having consumed two cups of coffee and a huge bucket of buttered popcorn, I still struggled to keep my eyes open while watching Harry Potter's *The Half Blood Prince* and *The Deathly Hallows* movies. Anthony finally fell asleep at 2:00 AM, but then I could not sleep at all, as on so many other nights in the life of a mother with a special needs child.

Almost comatose, I sleepwalked into my son's room the next morning and watched him slumbering like an angel. I gazed up at the ceiling, asking for strength, patience and most of all, some positive news.

I kissed him on his forehead and told him, "Sorry buddy - I know you're tired, but today's the day."

He gave me his drowsy-but-determined look. "I'm taking Yoda with me to keep me company while I take my test."

I told him what was always in my heart, "You are the bravest boy in the entire world and such a trooper! Yoda and Luke Skywalker will never be as brave as you."

With a great big smile, he rose out of bed, kissed me on the cheek, asked for help getting dressed, and told me he was starving (as usual).

I needed to scurry now, rushing to wash my face, brush my teeth, fix my hair, and apply a fast lick of lipstick. Running into my bedroom, I passed my husband in the hallway and realized that he was not only ready to leave, but that he had already had his coffee! He reminded me what I already knew... that I had 15 minutes to get ready and out the door.

He made another familiar pronouncement: "What's taking you so long?"

Don't you just love men? Here is where my patience must kick in.

Counting to ten, I calmly instructed him, "Please go to the Indian Chief Deli and pick up egg sandwiches to eat in the car, since you seem to have more time than me."

Once I heard the front door close, I put on my shoes, took my medications and remembered to let Jake out for his "morning constitutional." While he was outside, I filled up his bowls with water and dog food. Next I needed to give Anthony, Jr. his medications. As I heard Jake barking, my husband rang the front door bell with the egg sandwiches in one hand and coffee in the other. I checked my purse to make sure I had his written prescription, our insurance card and enough quarters for the meter in front of the hospital. Anthony was dragging Yoda out the front door, followed by my husband. I was left to lock up.

We arrived at the admitting desk around 7:30AM for his 9:00AM appointment. While we were waiting to be called, I took some time for morning prayers. As I was about to finish, I heard them call my son's name.

The administrator intoned, "You know the procedure - all paperwork needs to be filled out before we proceed to the Neurology Department."

Although we had done this on a number of occasions, I had knots in my stomach and an instant tension headache, most likely from sleep deprivation.

The EEG technician greeted us, glanced at Anthony's hospital bracelet, and said, "Room 404."

My son was holding Yoda tightly, but he resolutely climbed onto the hospital bed. Before closing his eyes, he assured me in a soft whisper, "Mom, it's going to be OK."

The technician asked him to lie still while he glued approximately 20 electrodes to his head and then wrapped it with gauze in the shape of a hat. This allowed the technician to look at his brain activity from the monitor. Since it was an ambulatory EEG, we were able to take him home with a portable electroencephalogram to observe any seizure activity throughout the day, at night, and during sleep. While he slept in our bedroom, my husband and I took turns monitoring him.

The next morning, Anthony tapped me on the shoulder at 7:00AM after his special night of watching movies, playing board games, reading books, and being given back rubs and leg massages. He enjoyed leg massages the most because of the cramps brought on by his seizure medication.

Of course, he wanted the electrodes out of his head immediately. "Please Mom- now!"

At the kitchen table, I realized he had gathered a plastic bag for the electrodes, nail polish remover, and cotton to remove the glue, and a separate bag for the electroencephalogram. In a nanosecond, it dawned on me how grown up he had become.

He sat expectantly at the kitchen table, waiting for me to begin the familiar procedure.

After the first seven electrodes had been removed, he demanded in a very loud and annoyed voice, "How much longer?"

This question was repeated until after the tenth and last time, when I was able to finally say, "OK - all done."

He sighed loudly, "Holy crap, Mom, that's freaking torture!"

It is important to remember that Anthony was a child that had had an 80% processing delay and could barely put full sentences together only a few years ago. Now he was able to put entire sentences together and use select curse words (if not all) in proper formation. I never thought I would be able to describe my oldest son as a typical teenager.

At this point, my husband needed to return all the testing data and material to the hospital in order for Anthony's EEG report to be read by his neurologist. We usually do not get the results back for at least seven to ten days, if not longer. However, I was in no hurry to yet again be told that his EEG was still showing spikes continuously throughout his day and while sleeping. Over the years, his EEG results have never showed any signs of improvement.

On March 13th, the neurologist called me with the results. She said the EEG showed no spike activity during the day, only while sleeping.

I took a deep breath and asked, "Excuse me, can you please repeat that?"

Her voice swelled with satisfaction as she repeated, "I am happy to inform you that there have been significant improvements with his brain activity throughout the day."

She went on to explain that he could also, in time, outgrow the abnormal spike activity during sleep, once his body went through puberty and his brain was fully developed.

After hearing these unexpectedly positive results, I became so emotional that I could barely breathe or speak. I quickly called my husband to give him the good news. He choked up and could not believe what I was telling him. Knowing in my heart that his feelings as Anthony's parent could only mirror those of my own, I was certain he was tearing up. I always knew my husband suffered silently because of our child's disabilities. Yet, he was unable to voice his inner disappointment and worries for his son's future out loud.

Holding back tears, he softly told me, "Honey I love you - talk to you when I get home."

My next step was to call the rest of my family and friends with the wonderful and hopeful news. After these calls were made, in the midst of all the excitement, I remembered that I needed to prepare dinner.

Thank God for Grandma Angela, who had given me some sauce with meatballs. All I needed to do was boil the ravioli. My younger son Michael and I ate dinner, made a plate for my husband, checked Michael's homework, and prepared him for school the next day. My husband walked in at the usual time, hugged me and said,

> "I know I don't tell you often enough, but you're a great mom! I guess miracles do happen. Thanks for always having faith, having patience, and being positive in what sometimes seems to be a hopeless situation."

I was beginning to think that maybe... just maybe... everything was going to be OK.

CHAPTER 7

"Knowing When You Need Help And Knowing When to Ask For It"

My Appointment with J. Lo

*W*hen Anthony, Jr. left our home, it was one of the darkest moments in my life. I remember sleeping with his light blue bunny sweater under my pillow. I cut one off one of the rabbit ears on the hood so I could carry it in my pocketbook. I would cry in the shower every morning so that no one would know my heart's devastation. My daily ritual became lying on the bed in a fetal position, crying until I had no more tears left, and remaining like that for hours on end. The truth was that I was unable to sleep unless I took something at night to help me. My own parents and brother were at odds with my decision and the separation from them broke my heart. I was slowly dying inside, but it was crucial that I get my act together for my son Michael and my husband Anthony.

My neighbor and friend Laura urged me to go for counseling. She explained how sometimes in life, no matter how strong you think you are, you need a professional to help you cope with this thing called "depression." I felt like nothing was important anymore; I was so tired and so sad that just getting out of bed was difficult. I was not really living; I was simply surviving.

When I met the social worker for my first appointment, I knew she would become a good friend. She instinctively understood how I felt and empathized with what I was going through: my struggles and worries as a parent over my sons' futures, my gut-wrenching guilt over moving Anthony, Jr. out of our home, the increasing distance between my husband and me, and my anger as a parent of a disabled child. From her, I learned that forgiveness can be a very powerful tool in the healing process. Once you are able to forgive yourself and others, you can experience something called "peace within your heart."

I continued to see her for a couple of months, and then she introduced me to a clinical psychiatrist. He immediately impressed me because he focused on the real issues, spoke truthfully, and did not waste my time. Not only was he a good listener, but he also gave sound advice. He said that what I was going through was "normal," but that I was like a train going full speed ahead with no brakes. Sooner or later, I was either going to crash or run out of fuel.

He told me that, "Sometimes in life we a need a little help - and it's alright to ask for it."

This would not be easy for me because I had always helped myself and did everything on my own. In other words, I was Miss Independence! He assured me that supervised medication would help me overcome my depression and so he prescribed Zoloft, which shortly made me feel myself again. What a huge difference it made!

These sessions of self-discovery led me to realize that when a mother felt an unconditional love for her child, she was capable of putting her child's needs before her own. I also discovered that the acceptance of your child's disabilities was the key to accepting help when you needed it, and that difficult choices did not come without consequences. The hardest lesson I had to learn was to forgive myself and others in order to achieve an inner peace.

However, I also learned that the path I had chosen was not an easy one for me, my husband, or those around me. I can now say that this ongoing experience definitely strengthened my human spirit and gave me the insight to recognize my choices as stepping stones towards a healthy family. The emotional pain cultivated an inner strength for me to become a leader and a voice for those children who cannot speak for themselves. Yet, although my intuition insisted that I needed to make this unselfish decision, that feeling alone did not make it all OK.

For those of you who struggle to raise your special children and feel it is nobler to suffer in silence, remember you are not alone on your journey. You have partners, i.e., other parents in the same situation. Please reach out to those parents and don't be afraid to admit you need professional help to live with your heartache.

CHAPTER 8

"If It Looks Like a Bully, and Acts Like a Bully, It's a Bully!"

The Bus Ride Showdown

*J*une 10th, 2011 started off like any other day. Michael's alarm rang at 8:00AM; he washed his face, brushed his teeth, dressed, and ate his breakfast. He was so excited because school was almost out for the summer. He was in 4th grade at our local elementary school. The bus pulled up to our home at approximately 9:05AM that morning.

However, despite the seeming normalcy of his morning routine, since March, Michael had been coming home emotionally distraught from numerous incidences that had been occurring on the bus ride to and from school. I reported it to the bus driver, the principal and vice principal, only to have my complaints fall on deaf ears. The principal's plan consisted of calling "trustworthy children that always tell the truth" into her office and then accepting their stories as fact. Fearful of repercussions and losing their jobs, the bus monitors would not defend my son during these attacks. These bullies consisted of eight students in the 6th, 5th, 4th and 3rd grades that would call Michael awful names, as well as hitting, punching, and cursing at him. This behavior was allowed to continue every day from early March up to mid-June. The abuse was everywhere: while Michael boarded the bus, exited the bus, walked in the hallways and had recess on the playground.

I decided it was time to take matters into my own hands. We purchased an iPhone that could take clear video and record voices. I instructed Michael to start recording whenever he felt threatened, whether it was cursing, hitting, or something worse. On a number of occasions, he would call me from the bus and ask me to listen. It was awful to have to hear firsthand what my son was going through, but at least now I knew I would have the proof I needed to go forward.

My stomach would churn every time I saw him board that accursed bus. I longed to defend Michael because, as parents, our instincts are to protect our children. Yet, I also knew that eventually he would have to learn to defend himself. Each day, I anxiously waited at the bus stop, not knowing in what condition Michael would arrive home. This particular day, he ran off the bus in hysterics, unable to breathe or finish his sentences. He made his way up my front stairs, pulled up his shirt and showed me an angry bruise in the shape of a boot heel on his upper left stomach area. I became enraged!

In the midst of all the hysteria, the vice principal called. She began the conversation by telling me she had just received a disturbing phone call from the parent of a second grader who reported that Michael pushed him on the bus today.

Given my mood at the time, my knee-jerk response was, "You need to get your story straight because it was my son who was kicked in the stomach by that same 2nd grader! What's more, I have photos and videotapes of all of the bullying that has been carried out on that bus against Michael. My husband and I will be in your office at 9:00 AM tomorrow to show you the photos of his latest bruise as well as other photos and videotape. Enough is enough! These incidents must stop. As you well know, this abuse has been going on since March of this year."

When my husband arrived home that night, I knew that I needed to remain calm while I related to him what had happened. If I could not keep my emotions in check, my husband would definitely be out-of-control at the school. I prayed for calmness and the ability to somehow ease my surging anger. I knew that I would need my total inner strength for the battle ahead of me. We let Michael sleep in our room, but it was a fitful sleep accompanied by night sweats, anxiety attacks, nightmares, and downright fear of what would happen to him on the bus and at school the next day. This would be the one of many such nights that we would have to endure until the situation would be finally resolved.

The next day he stayed home. In good conscience, I could not permit him to step foot in that school until someone was held accountable for what had taken place on that bus. My husband and

I entered the principal's office, and were greeted by her, the vice-principal, and the Superintendent of Transportation. Of course, I was prepared for the typical bureaucratic response to all parental complaints: The bus driver was not responsible because she had to keep her eyes on the road; the transportation company was not responsible because they are contracted outside the school; the school was not responsible because the bullying happened off school grounds.

My response could only be: "WHAT?"

We then played the videotape for them at full volume. I could not even bear to watch it. A single tear ran down my cheek and for once, I was actually speechless. They suggested separating Michael by having him sit in the front of the bus, while the bullies sat in the back. I argued that that would be victimizing the victim. Next they suggested that his bus be changed, which meant that the school authorities were either unwilling or unable to change the bullying situation. Their only solutions were to change Michael's seat or his bus.

The absurdity was such that I demanded that the parents of the students shown bullying on the videotape be notified of the occurrence and be held responsible their children's actions. The extent of their response to the situation was only that the child who kicked my son would be taken off that bus and not be allowed to attend any year end festivities. I then questioned the bus driver's experience, inaction, and negligence by not stopping the bus while my son was being assaulted. They repeated the same excuses I had heard earlier. Since I felt this meeting was getting us nowhere, I requested an immediate meeting with the superintendent of our school district.

At this point, despite my being emotionally exhausted, I was mentally preparing myself for the next strategic step. I would do whatever it would take to protect Michael because to see him like this was killing me inside. It was time for a quiet prayer for guidance. My faith is my secret weapon. It strengthens me not only for battles such as this, but also helps me to live this life in a spiritual way for the sake of myself and my family.

After praying, my next step was to give my body a bit of pampering in the form of a mani-pedi at my favorite nail salon. As I relaxed in the pedicure chair, a friend I hadn't seen in a while sat next to me. We began to catch up with each other's lives and I felt I could share my current crisis with her. Without getting into details, I gave her a summary of Michael's ordeal. A longtime active advocate for her two children, she advised me to contact a firm she knew that provided professional advocacy services for children and their parents to obtain the programs and services that best meet the needs of the child. I felt that an angel in disguise had sat down next to me that day to have a pedicure. She provided me with the information I needed to put me on the right path to help my son.

When I returned home, I made my phone call to the agency. My angel was right; these ladies were not only knowledgeable, but they also brought a fresh perspective. I was aware that I was too closely involved to see things clearly. I needed their expertise and professional support and so I asked them to attend the school district meeting with me.

During the conversation, I provided details about the bus incidents as well as the school's response. I described Michael's social "blindness," along with his inability to understand certain everyday situations or read body language and interact socially. She asked me if I had ever heard of Asperger's Syndrome. When she said those words, something clicked inside of me. How I cried on the phone! It was as if she knew my son better than I did. For some time, I had been tormented by the fear that something was amiss with my child, a fear that is hidden deeply inside of every parent and often disregarded. Asperger's Syndrome/Autism Spectrum Disorder (ASD) is characterized by significant difficulties in social interaction, alongside of restricted and repetitive patterns of behavior and interests. It differs from other autism spectrum disorders by its relative preservation of linguistic and cognitive development. Although not required for diagnosis, physical clumsiness and atypical use of language are frequently reported. Since I had one child under the Autism Spectrum, it made sense to have the other tested, especially when the siblings are boys. I should have known better.

The following day, I had a spiritual breakdown, which is very different from an emotional one. I was going to go food shopping, but I made a detour into the parking of lot of my parish. I believed that speaking to a priest and asking why this would happen twice in one family would help me sort through my feelings of despair and isolation. After all, I had one child with Pervasive Developmental Disorder/ Autism that I heartbreakingly surrendered to an agency residence and now I feared that my younger son had Asperger's Syndrome. I spoke to the priest, who listened intently and gave me a mother's blessing. He asked me to read the "Footprints in the Sand Prayer." Afterwards, I came to realize that I was truly not suffering alone or in silence, but that I was being carried on my journey with my children. We prayed together; I cried for two hours straight, scratching the corneas of my eyes with my contacts. Yet, believe it or not, I did feel an amazing peace come over me.

I was now prepared for the meeting, emotionally, spiritually, and mentally. A few days prior to the meeting, Michael had been tested, observed and diagnosed by a child psychologist, with not only with having Asperger's Syndrome, but also as emotionally disturbed by the bullying, which led to his having Post Traumatic Stress Disorder (PTSD). Now I could present this medical confirmation to my school district.

Our meeting date with the school district took place in the superintendent's offices. We had downloaded the bus video onto a computer screen. As we entered the boardroom, it was so quiet that one could hear the proverbial pin drop. Both advocates sat down to face the panel. One would type the meeting notes on her i-Pad as the other introduced the important topics of discussion. Seated at the table were the Superintendent of Transportation, the District Office Counsel, the Superintendent of Academics, the Assistant Superintendent, and the principal.

After listening to my complaints and utter disappointment at the lack of action taken on my son's behalf, the office counsel asked me, "Since there are only two more weeks left of school, what do you expect us to do at this late date?"

She then pointed to the number of people at the meeting as proof of their concern. I pointed out that my concerns were first introduced back in March, but had not been taken seriously until matters had escalated to such a point that I had no recourse but to take this next step.

After viewing the video of the assault, the transportation superintendent's opinion was that my son had provoked the altercation with his iPhone. He felt that the children were agitated because they did not want to be videotaped. I took a deep breath and pointed out that criminals also do not want to be videotaped when they are committing a crime.

I went on,

> "Would you prefer that he bring a gun instead of an iPhone to school for protection? I am using the same skills I learned from working on Wall Street to protect my son...a clear, well-conceived strategy to achieve my ultimate goal – a safe environment for the students. I should think that goal would be shared by the school administrators as well!"

As I expected, my argument silenced his ignorance.

Towards the end of the meeting, the advocates requested a private bus for my son, adding that we would get back to them with a full list of requests. More importantly, they instructed the educational administrators on how bullying could be handled without victimizing the victim. In closing, they gave a subtle, yet clear message, which was that our intention was to keep this episode private because we felt that the parents living in that district would not be comfortable with the way in which their children were being transported to and from school. They finished by advising the education officials that they would soon be hearing from us. I felt not only vindicated by what had transpired, but also confident in the team of advocates by my side. I no longer felt alone.

When I came home, my son Michael looked at me and said, "Mom it feels great to know you always have my back. That school now knows that you are no pushover! I love you Mom."

He then gave me a big bear hug, followed by "Mom you're the best!"

It was all the reward I needed and would serve to sustain me for the struggles yet to come.

CHAPTER 9

"Our Family Vacation to Disney World"

Where Dreams Really Do Come True!

*O*h happy day... Disney here we come! Our goal as a family was to take a well- deserved family trip to Orlando when Anthony had reached his IEP (individual education plan) goals. His dream was to go to Universal Studios to visit the Wizardly World of Harry Potter. That day had finally arrived and I started to make vacation plans.

Our first step was to fly to Orlando, Florida. During the security check-in, we needed to remove our shoes before walking through the detectors. My son Anthony refused to take off his shoes, arguing that he had nothing hidden in them, but that he would remove his shoes if the airport security attendant removed his as well.

He insisted, "It was a stupid law and that his feet did not smell!"

It is difficult enough to explain this procedure to children (and even some adults!) that do not have special needs, but imagine having to justify this odd ritual to a child with autism. We needed to pull Anthony aside and have a compassionate security screener spell out why he needed to remove his shoes. What finally convinced him to go along with the instructions was the fact that if he did not, we could not go to Disney to meet Mickey Mouse and all of his friends.

We finally arrived in Orlando's airport and next we needed to locate the Disney Express, which would take us and our luggage to our hotel. We had decided it would be best to stay at the Polynesian Resort so that we could be near the Disney tram in case of an emergency. The intense heat in Florida during the summer months caused us to be concerned that Anthony would suffer from heat exhaustion or seizures. The Polynesian Resort, with its two spectacular pools and landscaping of shady palm trees, was an absolutely perfect oasis for us. The only problem was that my husband had no sense of direction and so he kept getting lost going to and from our room. On the other hand, Michael has an incredible photogenic memory and sense of direction. My husband was constantly becoming frustrated by the fact he was always walking in circles; the more Michael tried to teach him the correct route, the madder he would become. It was so bad that he would tip the staff on the golf carts to drive us to and from the tram!

Anthony Jr's face at Harry Potter's Amusement Park was priceless.

His reaction made us believe along with him that we were in the presence of real wizards and warlocks. It is an amazing place to visit if you are a Harry Potter fanatic like Anthony. We spent the entire day at Universal Studios enjoying all the rides, drinking Butter Beer, and eating lunch at The Three Broomsticks.

I appreciated the staff's kindness and expertise in their interaction with special needs children. They gave us family fast passes because of the disabilities, which meant that we didn't have to wait on the seemingly endless lines in the heat, but instead were given access to a secret entrance. How cool was that!

The next day we visited Disney's Magic Kingdom (what an appropriate name for that place!) We were having lunch to celebrate Michael's belated birthday when suddenly Snow White and her Seven Dwarfs knocked on the glass window and asked the boys if they wanted to play hopscotch. Anthony was definitely not going to miss out on playing hopscotch with characters he'd always dreamed of meeting. If that wasn't enough of a dream-come-true experience, along came Cinderella and Little Bo Peep to join in the game. He couldn't believe his eyes! My heart danced with happiness knowing that he was so excited and happy. Autism did not exist for that one magical moment.

After lunch we decided to go back to the hotel for a well needed nap, planning to return for the Electric Parade that night. Unable to find his way to the right exit, my husband became exasperated. Michael coolly explained to his father that we were in the back of the Magic Kingdom Castle and that we just needed to go to the front, and then follow the brick path to the exit. It was hysterical to see my husband sitting on a bench, worn out by exhaustion, acting like a big kid who just wanted to go home because he was tired of being lost. I remembered how concerned I was about our children having meltdowns, but it was my husband who became overwhelmed, overheated, and confused by all the outside stimulation. I had to smile inside.

Despite my husband's temporary regression, we all had a

wonderful and unforgettable family trip. Most people expect to encounter difficulties when traveling with typical children, but try to imagine the worries and stress that are involved in traveling with special needs children. In addition to the emergencies (both medical and non-medical) that are part and parcel of every special needs parent's life, we had to maintain a strict schedule, be organized down to every minute detail, make sure all the medications were packed and a back- up plan for *just-in-case*! As a concrete example, Anthony had to be on eight pills a day for ten days of traveling...that's eighty pills to pack in a carry-on bag.

Yet, despite all of these precautions against the what-ifs of travel, I urge all of my fellow parents to not give up on your dreams because we did finally make it to Disney World... *Where Dreams Really Do Come True!*

CHAPTER 10

"The Heart of the Game"

Michael's Diagnosis with
ADHD and the Mustangs

*A*s Anthony adjusted to his new life, my family settled into a period of normalcy, peace and happiness, but that soon passed as we turned our attention towards Michael. We knew that Michael was intelligent, but he was having a hard time fitting in socially. He limited his relationships to only one friend at a time. He did not think or behave like a typical 11-year-old, but rather like a stressed out adult who was emotionally crippled by a heightened sense of anxiety that often culminated in severe migraines. At times, he spoke inappropriately to teachers, family, and friends. He innately understood that he was different from many of his peers. As a parent, I was becoming increasingly concerned because sociability is a vital part of daily life. I came to the realization that something was not quite right, but I was not ready to face that reality. Denial becomes a safe haven for anyone who is not prepared for the truth. I had been blaming Michael's lack of social skills on our family situation, which had caused me to shower his brother Anthony with so much help and support.

So, when Michael announced that that he wanted to play football on the town team, I was absolutely elated. He had been on their wrestling team for a while, but had decided to stop due to the panic attacks caused by the lack of control he felt. Now he wanted to play football. I was well aware that this was a brutally tough contact sport, but if this was what he really wanted to do, then we needed to support him. It definitely helped that his friend Colin also wanted to play football and would be on Michael's team.

During the week, he signed up for the football team; on Saturday afternoon we went for tryouts on the field. All the boys were so excited to be given their football equipment and jerseys. All that was needed now was a crash course on how to properly wear it all. Of course, on the first day of practice, my husband and I went with Michael behind the football shed to check whether he had been able to correctly put on his football gear. It was a good thing that we did because the only piece of equipment he was wearing suitably was his jock strap!

I had informed the coaches that Michael had ADHD and was on prescribed medications. Inwardly, I felt that this was an incorrect diagnosis, but I chose not to follow my instinct for once. He wanted to play football so badly that I could not bring myself to end his dream. The first problem that came up was that he only would play the position that was next to Colin. Then, Michael was rigidly determined that everyone on both teams had to follow the rule book to the letter. Michael was adamant: Rules, rules, rules were not meant to be broken! Any deviation from those rules (for example, the wrong call on a play) would send him over the edge. If someone called him a foul name, which happened on a number of occasions, Michael could not handle it. If the coaches were hard on him, he would shut down for the duration of the practice or the game.

We live in a very competitive sport community, but do the coaches and the parents have to be so obnoxious and aggressive? We were fortunate enough to have very patient coaches that really cared about the children, but a few of the other coaches were absolute fanatics about the outcome of these games. They would teach these young boys to play dirty. "Win, win, win," was the rallying cry and so the score, not sportsmanship, became all that mattered to them.

One fall evening, Michael had a football game on a school night. His pre-game anxiety was even more evident than usual. I could see from the way he was playing defense that something was not sitting well with him. I thought that perhaps the wrist he had broken a few months earlier made him apprehensive about playing such an injury-prone sport. In actuality, that was not the case, but I would have my answer to that puzzle a few years later.

That night, he ran off the field, screaming and yelling that he no longer wanted to play football because it was just too savage a sport for him. I must admit that my first reaction was one of disappointment. Finally, one of my sons was on a sports team just like other boys and it was an awesome feeling while it lasted. I felt as if I were living a normal life for a change. That feeling of being just like every other family had eluded me once again.

That night, I decided to stop being so overprotective because it certainly wasn't benefiting Michael. Children need to be independent and make decisions on their own. They need to learn to engage and connect on their own because there are unintended consequences of our overseeing their every move. Quite simply, we are around them much too much of the time. They need to become more responsible for themselves.

What I have learned as a parent from this experience is that the 24 hour media cycle focuses so much on the dangers and risks of childhood…risks and dangers that I don't remember growing up with when I was a young girl. As a result, we put our children in a protective parental bubble, creating play dates and choosing their range of activities to an excessive level. We rush to save them from any type of hurt, which slows down their ability to develop the life skills needed to navigate any future hardships. We praise them much too often and easily, and, in their need to feel deserving of that lavish praise, they fear disappointing us. We need to let them fail and experience disappointment. They will get over it! What they won't get over is the effects of being overly indulged by parents who want to act as their friends. Let them stand up and fight for what they really value in life on their own. If we treat them as delicate children, they will grow up to be delicate adults. We must prepare them for the real world that awaits them.

It's a tough world out there! Prepare your children for what lies ahead by providing them with a solid foundation that is built upon realistic expectations.

CHAPTER 11

"My Baby Leaves Home"

Unconditional Love and a Broken Heart

*J*t was a bitterly cold day in January 2008. Despite the bleak landscape, I was in high spirits, driving down a neighborhood street, listening to Journey's "Greatest Hits" CD. (This used to be one of my favorite collections, but now a deep sadness washes over me whenever I hear one of those songs.) The CSE Chairperson from our school district called me on my cell to say that there was something she would like to discuss before our meeting on March 25th. She added that, although she recognized that my husband and I were trying our best with Anthony, it would be in everyone's best interests to consider that he may need 24 hour supervision, with his medications monitored, in a less restrictive environment...in other words, a facility where he would learn and live outside of his home. Her tone was compassionate, but my mom-radar was giving off a warning.

Of course, I immediately reacted: "No I can't do that -are you crazy? He's only nine years old! He's still a baby!"

She calmly explained, as she must have done for countless mothers before me, that he was a danger to himself and others, and, more ominously, that we really did not have all that much of a choice. She went on to point out that the situation would only become more complicated as he got older, that his current situation was not the best placement for him, and that a transition of this kind would become more difficult for Anthony the longer we waited. She asked me to discuss all of these factors with my husband and to have him present at the next IEP meeting. The conversation left me numb, reeling with hurt, anxiety, and fear.

How did she come to this conclusion? I remembered the day, a few weeks earlier, when Anthony's teacher called me to report that he was having an extremely difficult day. He could not be controlled and, as a result, needed to be supervised in their padded room. This is a room where emotionally distraught students are placed so they cannot harm themselves or others. Worried and nervous, I feared that I would not reach my son fast enough; I do not even remember driving to his school. When I arrived, I went straight to his classroom and was met by the principal. We walked to the padded room, with my head spinning, my hands trembling, my heart racing, and my mind not knowing what to expect at this point.

The aide opened the door, and there stood my son looking pale, with his eyes glazed over. He had soiled his pants and had thrown up all over himself. I was not only sick to my stomach at what had been done to him, but also incensed by their callousness. I wondered how such treatment could be permitted. Then and there, I made the decision to bring Anthony home with me and not ever to return to that place. We never looked back.

However, his teacher there was not only passionate about working with special needs children, but also very insightful. Her first priority was always her students, not giving a damn about the backlash. Throughout it all, she gave me positive words of encouragement and excellent advice. She called me "the bulldozer mother" because I simply refused to give up and never stopped trying to help my son. I would demolish any and all obstacles that got in my way. Yet, both she and I knew it was time for him to move on, and that this chapter in his life was over. The next question for us was where to go from here.

When my husband came home from work that night, I told him we needed to discuss something really important. Woodenly, I sat with him, trying to find the right words to tell him what I knew would hurt him so deeply. He asked what was wrong, but the words just would not come out of my mouth. So I repeated the telephone conversation I had had that morning, word for word. He became confused and asked me to repeat what I had said.

When my words finally sunk in, he responded in the same way I had done earlier: "No way! He would live where?"

In my mind, I knew we needed to do more research with the school district to arrive at the right answers to our questions, but I also felt that our lives were about to change dramatically.

The CSE Chairperson called a few weeks later with the name of a nearby residence for us to visit. My husband and I were desperately trying to keep an open mind. It was a heart-wrenching process, but we knew we had to do what was best for our son. We looked at the day program and residential placement. The children living there ranged from those with severe impairments to those who were higher functioning, and included all types of disabilities. The news that the agency had an opening for him came all too soon. Since we were in an immediate need and knew the wait list for residential placement was years long, we decided to take it... despite our misgivings.

Although Anthony was no longer at the school, but home in my care, his former teacher continued to encourage me. She was a true blessing. The district had decided that he was to continue to receive services at home, but we first needed to stabilize his behaviors and emotions before the academic program could begin. To accomplish this, they sent a behavioral specialist from a private agency nearby. When she first entered my home to assess Anthony, he jumped from a chair onto my dining room table, grabbed the light fixture, screamed, and held a bowl of four hard boiled eggs in his hands, declaring that he was allowed to eat them all - just because he said so! She never blinked an eye, and I knew that another prayer had been answered when she walked through that door. She was intelligent, compassionate, insightful, and wise beyond her years because she knew exactly what my son needed, and that was private placement.

She told me that Anthony fit the profile of most of the children placed where she worked. She advised me to look into it and, if it matched my criteria, to put his name on the waiting list or speak with their social worker. I explained to her that my son had already been approved for the other facility because he needed immediate placement due to the urgency of our family situation. However, I told her I would keep her information for future reference just in case that residence did not work out. My intuition was in overdrive at that point.

Once we had made the decision, I cried every day and every night for weeks and months. Every moment was consumed by my dread of the conversation I needed to have with my son. However, from on high came an inspiration – his idol, Harry Potter! I sat down one night and told Anthony that he was going to Hogwarts School like Harry

Potter. He would learn to be a wizard and how to use a wand, and that we would visit him on the weekends.

He looked at me trustingly with his big warm brown eyes and said, "Great, Mommy, I can't wait!"

From that moment on, I knew that Harry Potter would become our magical transport. Every night, I kept myself busy by ordering furnishings online for his new room: a Harry Potter bedspread, sheets, pillows, owl, wand, lantern, sorting hat, costume, posters, etc… We had a Harry Potter everything! He was so excited and thrilled by this new adventure that I forgot my own pain for a while.

Then my husband and I attended his meeting on March 25th and were told that the placement would occur at the end of June. We left the meeting quietly thinking our own thoughts, but both choked by the heaviness that was in our hearts. I tried to keep my mind filled with positive thoughts every day.

One of the most stressful problems was how to tell my traditional Italian parents that their nine-year-old grandson was now going to live away from our home and, even worse, we would not be allowed to visit him for at least 60 days so he could better adjust to the new environment. As Anthony's parents, we were having a hard enough time wrapping our heads around this idea that had been so inconceivable to us just a few months earlier. Imagine what they, the older generation, would think? My head was telling me that I was doing the right thing for my child, but my heart was murmuring an entirely different story.

My husband and I did not speak very much to each other throughout the weeks before our son was to leave home. I feared we had reached a breaking point brought on by the heartbreak we were both undergoing. Each day, the distance between us grew further. I had always known that my husband was better at detaching himself from his emotions. This was a trait that I needed to develop in order to survive this ordeal, and now I knew that my husband would be the only one who could show me the way.

I was very fortunate to have my neighbor Lynn, who made many visits and phone calls to check up on me. She reminded me that Anthony eventually would be coming home for the weekends, and that this was not the worst thing that could happen to a parent. She was most likely remembering that her own son could never come home because he had died in a car accident when he was just 18 years old. To revisit that awful day took tremendous courage for Lynn. Her words made me realize that my situation was not as bad as those of other mothers. I empathized with her pain as never before and cried in her arms.

It came before I knew it: the weekend my baby was to leave home. We had finalized all of the planning. Grandma Frances was to stay over for the weekend to help ease everyone's anguish, especially Michael's. We had bought and labeled all of Anthony's clothing. We had packed all of his Harry Potter accessories and toys. It was time to go. Anthony grabbed my hand and with the other, held onto his baby blanket. Oh my God, was this going to be the absolutely hardest thing I ever had to do in my life?

We arrived at what was going to be his new home. His aunt and godmother were waiting to decorate his room and, most of all, be there for us. We brought in the boxes one by one. Like robots, we made his bed, put his posters up, put Hedwig the owl in the corner of his room, the lantern and wand on his night stand, and dressed Anthony up like Harry Potter.

He looked at us and said, "It's OK... you can go now."

I have been reminded on more than one occasion that these children feed off of other's emotions immediately. While trying to appear calm on the outside, inside I was being torn apart. I felt a pain I had never felt before in the middle of my chest... my heart was racing, my hands were shaking, and my eyes were swelling up. I had a choking sensation inside my throat and I could no longer utter a word. I was sad, angry, emotional, tired, guilty, anxious, depressed, nauseous and worried. Can a person safely experience all of these emotions at once without exploding?

My husband and I hugged and kissed him, and then it was time to leave him there. As we were walking out the door, we both instinctively turned around...he was still waving goodbye and smiling at us. My heart swelled with pride at his courage. My cousin and my sister-in-law were waiting for us. Once outside, we held each other in an intense group hug, succumbing to our held-in tears and pent-up emotions. Sooner or later, we knew we had to leave the parking lot, but not just yet. Finally we left, but only because we didn't want our first born son to see us hysterically crying. He wouldn't understand and might become frightened.

My husband prepared to drive away, but had to stop because he was crying with his head on the steering wheel. It was a very intense moment for me because I had never seen his raw emotions so openly in all the years I had known him.

He looked at me and asked the question he had kept hidden deep within him for a very long time, "Why my son? He's my namesake."

A brief moment later he confessed his worst fear: "If we make it through this, Cathy, we can make it through anything."

I echoed his sentiments silently within my heart.

As we drove away, my cousin, who had just left us a few minutes before, called to check on us once more. I tell her truthfully that I didn't know how I was going to make it through this. As always, she replied with words to comfort and encourage me:

> "You are the strongest woman I know and the best mother in the world. You both are making the ultimate sacrifice of letting him go because you have that unconditional love in your hearts, and you want what's best for him."

As you can tell, my cousin is one of my very special soul sisters, that female friend who tends to our inner needs. A soul sister keeps her eye on what really matters, even when we are distracted by life's little annoyances. She never questioned my decision to move Anthony to a specialized residence. She always knew exactly what to say and inspired me to do my very best. As a teacher for an inclusion (children with developmental delays combined with typically developing children) kindergarten class in Queens, she worked with children like my son on a daily basis. As a result, she was one of my few friends capable of seeing the full picture.

The drive home was a difficult one. I had such a pain in my chest; it was most definitely my heart breaking. I knew it was now time for me to sit with Michael and explain to this sensitive six-year-old boy that his brother needed to live somewhere else because of his disabilities. Once I had finished, he told me something that I already knew... that he didn't think it was fair that God shorted him a brother. To make it hurt less, I taped the most recent photo of them together to the inside front cover of his first grade marble notebook. That way, when he missed his brother and was sad in class, he could look at the picture and smile a little.

Finally, I was alone in my bedroom with only my thoughts to keep me company. I knelt on the floor, raised my hands and told God,

> "I'm releasing my son to you... please keep him
> safe, warm and wrapped in your arms. Please do this
> for me, and I shall continue to do your work and to
> serve those in need the best I can."

I put on my pajamas and lay in bed with tears in my eyes, torturing myself with the fear that Anthony thought we had abandoned him, and hoping and praying that no one would hurt him. Even though I was now already second- guessing our decision, I knew deep down in my heart that it would have been selfish and irresponsible to have kept him at home, making him more dependent on us. Yet sometimes when we pray for help, and receive the answer we know is right, we still don't like the response.

I knew I was not going to sleep at all that first night. I decided to go to the laundry room where I had left a pair of Anthony's pajamas that he had worn the night before. I made myself a warm cup of tea and slept with his Spiderman pajamas under my cheek so I could touch and smell them. I tormented myself with the idea that children usually leave home at the age of 18 when they are ready for college, not at Anthony's young age. How was I supposed to accept yet another abnormal situation in my life? Would this pain in my chest ever go away? My only comfort was my faith; I had to believe without question that I had made the right decision for my son. Was all this pain part of loving a child unconditionally?

The 60-day waiting period was like a life sentence... unending with no hope in sight. In the meantime, I needed to find the strength to reveal what had happened to my parents, knowing full well what their response would be. My parents were not only upset with our decision, but they were absolutely furious that we had not included them in this very serious family matter. At first, their outrage blinded them; they accused us of sending Anthony away because it was easier for us, both emotionally and financially. It tore my heart to hear that they would believe that of us. Didn't they realize that I needed them to help me through this crisis? As his mother, I always believed it was my job to take care of him, protect him and raise him, but the situation forced me to send him to live with actual strangers that I had to learn to trust with his well-being and upbringing! I was being torn apart in front of their eyes, but no one, not even my parents, could see my distress.

I was well aware of the close bond between my son Anthony and my mother. From the time he was born, she had watched him so that I could continue to work part-time in human resources for a brokerage firm in downtown Manhattan. However, it was now essential that she both acknowledge and understand that I was his mother. It was a very tough lesson for her. She called me every day like clockwork (sometimes more than once), and if she couldn't reach me at home, she was determined to find me on my cell phone. She informed me of their rights as grandparents, and warned me that I could not stop them from seeing him. It was her sorrow and sense of hopelessness that made her speak to me in that way.

At one point, she threatened us with a family court hearing to claim grandparents' rights. She involved my brother by crying on his shoulder, which made him sympathize with them, preventing him from recognizing the sacrifices we had had to make as Anthony's parents. Just when you thought things could not get any worse, somehow they just do.

May 28, 2008 was one of the most difficult days of my life. My husband and I had a court date for a preliminary proceeding in family court. I was seeking a court mandated order of protection against my parents and my brother. How had it come to this? When my husband and I finally agreed that Anthony needed outside residential placement and schooling, it was a very private and delicate situation. We knew what we had to do, and really did not wish to discuss the pros and cons with other people, even those closest to us. We knew that everyone would have their own opinions, but, in our fragile state of mind, we could not open the matter up to debate. It was just too painful a subject for us to rehash over and over again, and so we kept our decision secret until we ourselves had come to grips with it. Moreover, since my parents had traditional old-European beliefs, we believed that they would not only be unable to fully understand the complexities of his disabilities, but also that they would be unable to accept that their grandson had become a danger to himself and to others around him. In retrospect, that was a mistaken belief on our part. We had disrespected them by not trusting them.

So, when we brought Anthony to his new home, we decided to tell my parents about it only after the fact. I suppose it was not only my own sense of guilt that led me to think that this was the right move, but also my wish to shield them from the anguish I was going through for as long as possible. I knew that the ties were very close between my parents and my son. As such, I felt that this bond would make it more difficult for them to admit what was right in front of them, making it much easier for them to remain in denial. Why? The truth hurts too much. In other words, this decision to send Anthony to another residence was tantamount to admitting that we had failed him as a family. That was a tremendous burden to have lain upon their shoulders; I knew because I was falling down from the weight of it all.

However, the choice we had made not to keep my parents informed about Anthony's placement had serious repercussions. My parents and brother felt hurt at being left out of this decision and made those feelings clear in every conversation we had with one another. These family discussions continued for a few months, never letting up and only worsening as time went by. Fueled by anxiety and with my emotions running wild, I filed for court orders of protection against my parents and brother. A word of advice: never allow your emotions to take control of your actions. While it is true that we all have the free will to make a choice, it is also true that you cannot choose the consequences of that choice. As a result of my choice, summonses were served against my parents and brother, accompanied by manipulative lawyers, unnecessary legal fees, ugly court appearances, and a family torn apart by their deep and abiding love for this one child.

The day arrived for the preliminary hearing and I was sick to my stomach. I had a pounding headache brought on by anticipation of the coming confrontation at the courthouse. The family gathered in the waiting area along with our lawyers. We sat facing each other on opposite sides of the room. It was surreal. We were finally called into the courtroom. The judge had already reviewed the case file along with the five-inch stack of Anthony's records. She peered down at all of us and pointed out that from her observations, her opinion was that we did not belong there because we did not fit the typical profile of the petitioners present in her courtroom. She then instructed us to discuss the issues outside the courtroom, and come to an agreement together as a family with our lawyers present. Once we had finished, we were to come back to schedule a court date. Before we left, she asked my parents to look at me and ask themselves if I appeared to be calm, unconcerned, and not distraught over what was happening to my child and my family. In fact, I had been hiding behind my husband, holding back my tears, with fluttering hand movements, trying to control my oncoming panic attack.

The judge was wise because just by looking at us, she knew that we would come to an agreement regarding visitation rights for my parents. I could never have kept either of my children away from them. Not only had they always been loving parents to me, but it would have been an injustice on my part to try to break them apart. Ultimately, the judge showed us that it would have been very selfish for my husband and I to take that away from them. If we had not stepped into her courtroom that day, I believe my relationship with my parents and brother would have been irreparably damaged. I took a drastic step that I knew had to be taken to end a situation that was endangering my family unit. Sometimes we need to confront our fears head-on in order to abolish them altogether.

Over time, our family relationship was mended. The path was not an easy one, and there were many missteps along the way. However, we all worked at it because we knew that our efforts would eventually bring us closer together, with a better understanding as to the true meaning of family. My son Anthony needed us to be together as a family, now more than ever before.

In the meantime, my husband and I grappled with our own uncertainties, brought on by criticism from outsiders. We realized that only time would tell what improvements and setbacks were ahead for our child, but we had made the decision to take that chance for his future. We feared that we had cast him off into an unknown abyss, but our only chance of survival was to hope against hope that the choice we had made would give our son a life of independence, with no one but himself to rely on for his daily needs.

This is the life that parents of typically developing children take for granted; it is so difficult for them to truly appreciate how blessed they are to have a child that is able to go to school by bus without supervision, eat with utensils, bathe alone, do homework, have friends, play sports, communicate and express their emotions appropriately, with no medications required to function in the real world. In other words, I mean all of the everyday activities that most of the children like Anthony need to be taught consistently and routinely every day, with support from skilled professionals and often harried parents.

Even my best friend was upset and disappointed with me when I chose to place Anthony away from my home, refusing to allow me to discuss my feelings with her as well as the reasons why we had done what we had done. I needed a friend to just listen to my pain, but helping me find a way to survive during this darkest period of my life was the furthest thing from her mind. Instead, she asked if she could keep him and raise him, which felt like a slap in the face. Yet, I loved her for her offer because I knew that her heart was as broken as mine and this way her way of coping. It was simply her maternal instincts coming out. She never intended to hurt me, but clutched at the chance to raise my child since she was unable to have children of her own.

To this day, it still troubles me that most of the people I knew and loved could not understand that it was love that drove us to make this ultimate sacrifice and decision. Perhaps this was because it was the love that surpasses understanding, but the simple truth was that we did not have much of a choice. We had to be realistic and the reality was that, although he appeared to be absolutely perfect on the outside, only we, his parents, knew firsthand the debilitating disabilities that plagued his inner soul. The fact that his symptoms were not outwardly evident made it extremely difficult for others to agree with what they felt was an extreme measure on our part. They never realized that the situation had finally reached a point where his disabilities were becoming increasingly difficult for us to manage on our own. There were just too many doctors, too many decisions to be made, too many specialists to see, too many schools, evaluations, and IEP meetings… and Anthony was not getting any better!

I always say that family, friends and outsiders live the commercial, while my husband and I live the movie. They would spend holidays and a few hours with you and then - not only did they judge you, but they also believed that they had the antidote for all of your problems. Such well-meaning people should be gently reminded that children are not like shoes; if they don't quite fit, or are damaged, you cannot return your son or daughter for new ones, or better yet, ask for a refund! These children certainly did not expect to be born like this, nor did their parents. It just is what it is, but it will become what we choose to make of it. I knew that my son did not want to suffer with the mind with which he was born. I had to let go in order to help him!

Why were so many of my family and friends unable to see our despair at that time? I thought I would have a nervous breakdown from trying to save my family and my marriage. The divorce rate of parents of special needs children is 80% on average. I was well aware of that statistic, having seen it firsthand with other couples in our same situation. All of us were feeling miserable with only the slimmest of hopes to sustain us, which was that there had to be better days ahead.

In less than a year, Anthony left his first residence, which had been chosen because it was the only placement available at that time. The district felt, as did we, that he needed an immediate placement because he was in danger of harming himself and others. We had known that it was going to be just a temporary home for him because much of the population consisted of lower functioning children. That being the case, there was a serious lack of academics and technology in the school, two areas that Anthony required to improve his future lifestyle.

During this period, I had stayed in touch with the behavior specialist at the private school and had kept her abreast of my concerns with the original placement. She made a private appointment for us to look at the school and residential placement. I did this without the requisite permission from the school district because I didn't want to have to wait for them to go through the usual administrative and political machinations that would give me permission to obtain this appointment. I was tired of jumping through hoops, listening and waiting for no one.

After our visit, I informed the CSE Chairperson that I judged this agency to be the best place for my son and that they had a bed open and waiting for him. I knew from experience to explain the legitimate reasons why my husband and I felt he needed to be moved. In a few weeks, the final move took place. We packed everything from that first residence and moved Anthony to the place that my intuition told me would be right for him and for us.

At the conclusion of this chapter, which I wrote with great difficulty and an outpouring of tears at the memory of it all, I feel that it is my duty to remind those that are not walking in another person's shoes not to judge, comment, or even qualify themselves to understand someone else's decisions. If you haven't actually lived through a situation, whatever it may be, please realize that you have no right to second-guess what is being done. You are entitled to your opinion, but sometimes careless words have a negative impact... so my sincere advice is to keep them to yourself. Your inner thoughts really do not need to be expressed, and they may likely hurt the other person beyond measure as well as your relationship with them. Think before you speak and check your own misgivings at the door; thoughtless words always hurt, are never forgotten, and continue to have profound repercussions on those you love!

CHAPTER 12

"911"

Is Our Baby Going to be Alright?

*T*t was October 29, 2007 – one of those breathtakingly beautiful days that only occur in the fall. The air was crisp, the sun bright and the leaves had turned to those amazing hues of copper, purple, and bronze. It was the christening day of my cousin's newborn son…a day of hope and new beginnings. My boys were excitedly looking forward to spending time with their cousins. We were all so happy, never imagining the night to come.

As my husband was parking in front of the restaurant, I heard Anthony shout hello to his grandparents. Both of the boys could not run out of the car fast enough for some hugs and kisses. We climbed the stairway to the main dining hall and, as we passed the kitchen, the smell of fresh bread and Italian food was mouthwatering.

Michael looked up at me with his chubby cheeks and twinkling eyes to solemnly announce, "Mommy I want 'pasghetti' with lots of sauce and cheese."

We sat at the table with my parents, my brothers, their wives, and my four gorgeous nieces. My sons always enjoyed sitting in the middle of their girl cousins because they received so much love and attention from them. It was so nice to have everyone sitting at the table, eating delicious food and drinking Italian wine, while talking to each other a mile a minute! In the meantime, Anthony and Michael were having their own fun dancing and playing with their cousins. The best part was that we were all soaking in some quality family time for a change.

Shortly after the abundant meal, we were served espresso, cappuccino, fresh fruits, and a selection of Italian and Greek cookies. After all, what's a European celebration without the all-important Venetian Hour? There was a short moment during dessert when my son Anthony was taking a personal tour of the tables. Of course, a boy with the face of an angel was able to cajole the guests into giving him fresh watermelon from their tables. He returned to me licking his lips, with sticky fingers and watermelon seeds stuck to his face.

Grandma Angela took him to the bathroom to wash away the mess.

As they walked away, I heard my son say, "Grandma, my tummy hurts."

A short hour later, his eyes glazed over and his body suddenly appeared weary and overly fatigued. We quickly said our good-byes and left for home.

When we arrived home, Anthony had fallen into a deep sleep, so my husband placed him on the couch in the den and I brought Michael to his bed. I had undressed, but decided to catch up on some reading in the den in order to watch Anthony, Jr sleep.

After two hours, it was time to wake him for his 8:00 PM seizure medications. I remember thinking to myself that I hated to disturb him. All of a sudden I saw that his body was shaking violently, his eyes were rolling, and drool was oozing out of his mouth.

I screamed for my husband, "Anthony's having a grand mal seizure!"

My husband became white as a ghost, frozen in fear at the unfamiliar sight. My cries awakened Michael from his deep sleep. That was when my mind and body went into overdrive, rushing to place Anthony on his side and making sure that he would not bite his tongue. I silently prayed that he would be alright.

In the meantime, my husband's reflexes also kicked in. He called 911 and the emergency team was inside our home in a matter of minutes. Although his seizure lasted three to four minutes, the horror of it felt like an eternity; time stood still and all of the activity passed before me in slow motion. It was like one of those terrible dreams when you just want to wake up so that the nightmare would end.

When the seizures finally stopped, I had to jumpstart my husband back into reality. It was also critical that I comfort Michael because the look of fear and anxiety on his face was painfully obvious. At one point, I was actually afraid that the paramedics would also have to resuscitate my husband.

Knowing that Anthony would become frightened if he woke up in the middle of an ambulance trip, we decided to use a police escort while driving to the hospital in our own car. I wrapped him in a blanket and carried him in my arms just like I had done when he was a baby. I kept checking to see if he was breathing. On the way, I called my parents to meet us at the hospital to take Michael safely home with them.

In the emergency room, the staff ran blood tests to check his levels of medications. The emergency room doctor asked if he had eaten anything out of the ordinary that could have caused the seizures. I knew in the pit of my stomach that the likely catalyst to his grand mal seizure was the natural sugars in all the watermelon slices he had eaten at the party. Although I had no idea that a high amount of sugar could cause seizures, the guilt I felt as his mother flooded my senses like a strong and bitter pill. Even after all these years, I have never forgotten the feeling.

That night my husband and I brought Anthony home and he slept in our bed. We were both so shaken up that neither one of us slept. The next day we brought Anthony to the neurologist that had first diagnosed him with epilepsy and ADHD at the age of three. We waited patiently to be called, expecting the usual ninety minute wait. However, since it was an emergency visit, we did not have to wait that long. As we anxiously sat in front of him, the doctor reviewed the blood level test results from the night before.

After what seemed like an hour, he looked directly at me, and in an arrogant, loud, obnoxious tone, snarled, "How does it feel to be responsible for your son's first grand mal seizure?"

My husband was astounded: "Excuse me!"

The doctor shortly responded, "You heard me."

I was not surprised. Although this doctor had come highly recommended by my pediatrician, my intuition had made me wary of him from the moment we first met. He struck me as a cold person with no empathy at all for his patients - not a good trait in a pediatric neurologist that had to work with scared young children and their worried families.

I took a deep breath, looked him in the face and said the words that had been on my mind all of those years: "Just because you have that degree on the wall does not give you permission to speak to a mother like that! A good doctor has compassion and understanding for his patients."

Knowing my temperament, my husband stood between the almighty doctor and me. All my pent-up emotions were evident on my face. Since my son was sitting there, I controlled myself with the assurance that I would get even with this doctor by working to make sure that I and no other parent would have to undergo his abuse again. True to my word, as I walked out of his office, I asked for my son's file and told the nurses that Anthony would no longer be a patient there. I then proceeded to report his unprofessionalism to the New York State Medical Board.

Yet, that doctor's accusation had cut me deeply; the hurt, worry and pain were almost unbearable. I knew I had to put his sneering words behind me in order to give Anthony the help he needed. I prayed for the strength to forget and go forward.

I found that strength in the morning. I made a call to my trusted pediatrician who, after hearing about my experience, gave me the name of a new neurologist. I met with her the next day and she changed his meds, which has made all the difference for Anthony. She continues to monitor him to this day with skill, patience, and best of all, understanding.

CHAPTER 13

"The Stalking of Dr. Z"

Road Trip with My BFF

S o my BFF's name is Stephanie; she and her husband are Michael's godparents. She was one of the first people to hold both my children when they were born. She has never left my side, has always had my back and, most importantly, is forever the friend that has always been just a phone call away, no matter what. My nickname for her is "Pyramid of Information" since she is so intelligent and informative. She can come up with a fool-proof plan or solution to any dilemma in a matter of minutes (and sometimes seconds)!

We don't have to communicate with one another on a daily basis, but when we do touch base, we just pick up where we left off as if no time had passed. You know who I mean... *that* friend, the one who comes over in her pajamas, bunny slippers and robe to knock on your front door to make sure all is well. She was the one that went with me to the emergency room at midnight on the Sunday when my son dislocated his elbow. Even then, she eased my stress by making me laugh at the poor patient in the next bed who had glued her eyes shut with Krazy Glue. (She had mistakenly used it in the dark instead of her prescription eye drops.)

When I first thought there was something not quite right with my son Anthony, she never once questioned my apprehension. So many others pooh-poohed my mounting fear, but not her; she believed in my intuition. Like a second mother, Stephanie had recognized the signs for herself. Anthony was speech-delayed, his eyes became trance-like at times, and he occasionally drooled. He could never sit still, had no memory recall, had a hard time socializing with children his age, was defiant with his teachers, and had extreme separation anxiety.

Being the person that she is, Stephanie never left my side even while she was going through the difficulty of trying to conceive a child of her own. Some women are born to be mothers and she was definitely one of them. Unfortunately, without rhyme or reason, it just did not happen for her. Why is it that some women that should not have children are able to conceive, and some of the most deserving women cannot? I guess you could say some questions can never be answered. What happened to my dear friend was another example of one of life's awful mysteries.

As my best friend and confidante, Stephanie knew that I had been struggling with Anthony's development issues for quite some time. She reminded me about the session Anthony had had a few years earlier with Dr. Z, a prominent child psychiatrist. My son had shown great improvements after Dr. Z's evaluation and change in medications. She suggested it was time to take Anthony for a follow-up visit.

I called his phone number, only to learn that Dr. Z had relocated to another university upstate. I knew he was very much in demand, but I was a mom on a mission, desperate to make an appointment with him. I left numerous messages at his office. I refused to give up. Finally, he returned my call to explain that he was teaching students during the day. If I wanted to see him, it would have to be at the university after 3:00 PM. He also informed me that the fee would be $300 per visit, with no insurance accepted. Dr. Z also mentioned that he knew that if he did not meet with me, I would continue calling him until he did. He was most definitely correct! His expertise in psychiatry was clearly evident in his assessment of my utter determination.

My next step was to give Stephanie the good news. I told her the appointment details and, as usual, she was ready to go that day!

Her exact words were, "Confirm the appointment and don't waste any time. We need to do this now!"

On July 31st, 2007, Stephanie came to pick us up and we were on our way. She even made the ride there seem like a breeze. We made that same trip at least four times. She never complained about the traffic, never wanted any money for gas, and silently listened to my endless concerns and worries. I will always remember how, before one of the visits, Anthony had a yen for McDonalds just as we had arrived at the psychiatrist's office.

Instead of becoming exasperated, she looked at him with assurance and said, "I will find you one."

However, according to the security guard at the university, there was only one McDonalds in the area, which was located all the way on the other side of town with no easy access to parking. Stephanie was up for the challenge.

She made a U-turn out of the university parking lot and declared, "We have half an hour... I will find it."

I never doubted her word for a minute. In two blinks of an eye, Anthony had his Happy Meal, Auntie Stephanie got a huge kiss and hug, and we were on our way back to the office. I am convinced that she hides her Superwoman cape under her clothes.

On the last and fourth visit, we were to learn the diagnosis, be prescribed a change of medications, as well as a specific behavioral and daily living plan that was to be submitted to the school district. I always knew in my heart of hearts that there was a missing piece to my son. We were about to finally discover what that missing piece was.

I will never forget that last visit. We entered Dr. Z's office; Anthony was playing with blocks on the floor, while Stephanie and I sat across from him. Dr. Z handed me the plan of action, but was having a very difficult time reviewing the diagnosis with me.

I looked at him directly and said, "Dr. Z, we haven't come all this way not to know. Please tell me your analysis of Anthony without any more hesitation. I just can't take it."

He replied with some relief, "You are a no-nonsense kind of mother. I usually need to use kid gloves when speaking to parents in situations like these, but not with you."

He solemnly continued with the words I long dreaded, yet expected to hear: "My diagnosis is that your son has Pervasive Developmental Disorder...it falls within the Autism Spectrum."

Releasing the breath I had been holding for several years now, I shakily responded, "OK, at least now I know what I'm dealing with."

I was remembering all those evaluations that had been carried out in the years since Anthony was three years old, not one of them yielding the full truth. The wording was always tempered with "possibly" or "maybe."

I turned towards my friend who was sobbing uncontrollably. She was always known as the ice princess. She rarely cries, but when she does, she cannot stop.

She apologized for her outburst, saying, "I was supposed to be here to support you. My heart is breaking for you."

In the next breath, she demanded to know why I wasn't crying – me, who cries at Hallmark commercials! I felt a strange sense of calm mixed with relief, a feeling I had not experienced since I first heard my inner voice telling me that something was amiss with my oldest child. I felt vindicated, but more importantly, now I knew I had a concrete plan of action to follow.

As I explained to my sobbing friend, "It's better to know than not to know. Now I can begin to do what I have to do."

And that is exactly what I did...

CHAPTER 14

"The Greatest Little Surprise"

My Shadow's Name is Jake

*W*ho doesn't want a puppy for Christmas? My husband! Why? Well, dear reader, read on…

Whenever the subject of a family dog came up (and in our house, that question was raised on a regular basis), his response invariably was, "They are a lot of work, money, responsibility - and if something happens to the dog, it's heartbreaking for everyone. Besides, I know that I'm going to end up walking the dog and picking up after him."

My stubbornly optimistic reply: "If you love me and the kids, you would let us have a puppy!" I was not about to give up!

It was Christmas of 2006 when I first asked Santa for a puppy for Christmas and my husband said we needed to discuss it further. So that's exactly what we did. I went online and looked up some breeds. My perfect dog would not be too big, with a sweet temperament, intelligent, not hyper or a yapper, and, most important of all, had to be good with children. Why? Excluding the intelligence trait, the description of my perfect pet was designed to be the exact opposite of my children. If the puppy turned out to be anything like my children, I could see that my future fashion accessory would not be straight out of *Vogue*, but instead the very special white jacket. You know the one I mean… one size fits all, with the straps that tie your arms around you! A mischievous puppy that enjoyed barking all day and night would turn my home into the next "Amityville Horror House," if you know what I mean!

Despite my hidden fears, I was determined to forge ahead with my plan to bring a puppy into our lives. We started out on our quest to find the perfect pup, but there were so many stores and so little time! Every one of them boasted a full collection of small, adorable, playful, pooping and peeing puppies. Every weekend, we would visit several pet stores with my three "boys" in tow, including my husband as part of the trio. (You women know what I'm talking about.) We would pick out a few puppies, and an employee would bring them out, one at a time, into the meet and greet puppy play area. However, the trek that had begun as a fun family activity soon became tiresome as weeks turned into months.

Finally, in the fall of 2007 my husband asked (with a bit of impatience), "What exactly are you looking for in a puppy?"

I patiently explained the obvious to him by pointing out that no matter how many precious puppies we had met, none of them had been the right dog for us. As he stared at me further with a puzzled look on his face, I informed him that we would not be continuing our search. If it was meant for us to have a puppy, he would find us.

I heard skepticism in his next question: "How would he find us?"

I spelled it out for him: "Just like everything else. The big man upstairs knows what we want, and if this special puppy exists, our paths will meet."

Of course, his just-like-a-man response was, "OK, I get it - you're having a moment of clarity."

Christmas 2007 came and went, and still no puppy appeared. Three months passed and we were now in April. It was a beautiful spring day and I decided to go buy cold cuts at my favorite deli. As I was ordering, I ran into Ellen who worked for the school district in our area. She informed me that she was taking some time off to do something that had been her dream for many years. Then, she pulled out a pocket-size photo album of her new breed of puppies, totaling eight in all. I could not believe how beautiful they were! Six females and two males, each a blend of the King Charles Cavalier and French Poodle breeds, looked up at me appealingly from the photos. The one that captured my heart had curly beige hair with spots of brown, accentuated by spots of white on his head and paws.

With my heart in my mouth, I asked, "Does he belong to anyone yet?"

I was thrilled when she replied, "No, and isn't it funny that you picked the one male I have left?"

I called my husband from the store to announce that I had found the perfect puppy:

"In actuality, Anthony, like I told you, he found us. I'm taking the boys to see him tonight and leave a deposit."

He persisted, "How do you know he's the one?"

I pronounced with finality, "I just do."

I took down her personal information and told her we would be at her home around 6:00 PM that night.

The day could not have passed any slower. As soon as the boys came home from school, I told them my happy news. Now the boys were just as impatient as I was, so around 5:30 PM we headed to Ellen's home with our hopes and heads both held high. We rang the bell and finally Ellen answered the door. She told us that the puppies were upstairs being fed by their mom. We followed Ellen upstairs in quiet (at least for us) anticipation. In the room we found eight precious "Cavapoo" puppies resting in a feeding bed with their mom.

What a thrill it was for us! No sooner did I sit on the floor, when one of the puppies left his mother and began circling around my feet. He had beautiful brown eyes, a curly tail, and white spots on his paws and head. It was the puppy from the picture! I knew right then and there that he was meant to be our long awaited pet. He was so playful and sweet. Of course, I just wanted to take him home right then and there, but I knew that he needed to stay with his mom for a few more weeks.

Now that we had finally found him, it was time to shop for the newest member of our family. We made a beeline for Petco, buying him a bed, brush, puppy food, snacks, carrying case, harness and a leash. Of course, like most women, I hid the bill from my husband.

The prescribed four long weeks had passed, and it was time for us to pick him up. He had had his first round of shots and was healthy enough to leave the litter. My husband and I brought a baby blanket to keep him warm. It reminded me of those special, never-to-be-forgotten days when we carried each of our newborn sons home. I wrapped him in the baby blanket and he had his eyes closed. He was absolutely perfect! I felt joy swelling up within me.

That night, we had a family discussion on names and chose Jake, which means both "healer" and "most satisfactory." That was exactly what my family needed at that time. My son Anthony, Jr. was to leave our home that summer to live in his school residence, and along came

Jake in the spring of that same year. My family desperately needed some type of diversion to take our minds off of the pending move, and Jake was it. When I cried about the upcoming separation from my child, Jake lay consolingly at my feet, barking only when necessary. When the sadness bubbled up deep within my soul, he would kiss my hands and played patiently with my children. Jake followed me closer than my shadow, slept next to me on my bedroom floor, and cuddled next to me as I read a book or watched television. He needed me and I needed him. He saved my life! He was my joy and gift from Heaven, and carried me from one unconditional love to the next…

CHAPTER 15

"The Man in the Electric Blue Dodge Ram Truck with Bright Silver Rims"

Child Protective Services

*I*t was October 2006 and Michael had been attending kindergarten for the past month at our local elementary school. Anthony, Jr. was attending the local school for special needs children. I could not believe how quickly my boys were growing up...

Anthony's bus arrived at 8:45 AM, which was no guarantee that he would easily cooperate and board it. What did I mean by this? Well, he might have thrown down his knapsack, cursed, kicked, screamed, yelled, punched, bit, maybe have taken off his clothes or, worst case scenario, decided to run off as soon as he saw his bus coming. This scene would be repeated on a daily basis, meaning that every day I would awaken with my heart racing and my anxiety soaring through the roof because I never knew what to expect from Anthony's erratic moods and behavior. If there were no incidents during the morning pick-up, then I would await the dreaded phone calls from school during the day.

In harsh contrast, his brother Michael had excitedly put on his Spiderman knapsack, grabbed his lunchbox, and eagerly waited in the hallway for his bus. Considering all the chaos that goes on in our home, it was only natural that he would be happy to have a change of scenery. When his bus arrived, he grabbed my hand, kissed my cheek and ever so sweetly told me to be safe and have a nice day.

Anthony, on the other hand, found transitioning from home to school very difficult, which meant that the bus ride to and from school was pure misery for all concerned. The one and only saving grace was that the bus driver and matron demonstrated tremendous patience, compassion and care towards every child on that bus. We knew that they did not perform their job just for a paycheck. They loved what they did; it showed on their faces.

For parents of special needs children who have siblings, there is a pervasive feeling of guilt. We have to devote so much time and attention to the child with severe disabilities, constantly working with them, filling out forms, taking them to specialists and therapists, and remaining vigilant to their wants and requirements. In my case, I regretted that I never had the time to just sit with Michael and give him the one-on-one attention that he needed to learn the alphabet, numbers, reading, etc... As a result, he struggled with academics. Yet, although he often lived in Anthony's shadow, he has become very independent and quite mature because he had to learn to make it on his own.

Finally, after what seemed like forever, both my children were on their way to school. I turned my attention to my typical weekday regimen of washing breakfast dishes, refilling the usual prescriptions for my son, doing laundry, running errands, paying bills and preparing dinner. Since it was such a beautiful crisp autumn day, I wanted to finish as much I could so that when they arrived home we could have fun outside. The afternoon started as planned. We had been playing a great game of whiffle ball for at least an hour. Anthony displayed amazing strength when he hit that ball. It cleared houses upon houses. As he forcefully hit one of my pitches, I raced to retrieve the ball that had shot clear across the street. As I was turning to run back with it, I saw an electric blue Dodge Ram truck with bright silver rims pull up in front of our house.

A gentleman emerged from the truck, clipboard in hand.

As quick as a mother hen, I began running hurriedly towards my children when I heard him ask, "Which one of you is Anthony, Jr.?"

I knew to ask for some identification, and then learned he was with Child Protective Services. He was there because the agency had received a formal complaint of abuse from the school. He requested that we go into my home to prevent the neighbors from hearing our discussion. I asserted that I had nothing to hide, but went inside at his insistence. Once inside, he informed me that an aide in Anthony's classroom had noticed a black and blue mark on his leg and reported it to the school. He turned towards Anthony and asked my son to show him the bruise; he inspected it with microscopic intensity. Then he questioned and spoke to both my children separately.

Afterwards, he informed me that my husband could be removed from the home if the investigation confirmed that the bruise was caused by abuse. I tried to explain that my son Anthony had attempted to jump from one captain bed to the other while reaching for the ceiling fan. He fell down as my husband tried to catch him, banging his leg hard on the headboard as he tumbled onto his bed. My defenses were up:

"Do you have any idea what it is like to raise a special needs child?"

He stared directly at me and responded, "I'm not the one beating my kids."

I could not believe what I was hearing.

"You think we're beating our children?"

His tone of voice grew very loud and confrontational.

"Just because he's disabled doesn't mean you have the right to beat him!"

I was absolutely stunned - my insides churned in disbelief, followed by a deep sense of rage and nausea at what I had just heard.

As little as he was, Michael had the sense to seek out my neighbor Lynn who lived around the corner. He described a bad man talking to Mommy and that he said he wanted to take Daddy away. She immediately rushed into my home to question his authority and the reason for his visit. Outraged by his accusations, she defended me, saying that I was "a very attentive, loving, and caring mother that would never raise her hands to her children." She went on to say that my boys were very active, often injuring themselves as a result. She then advised him that he was in the wrong house and needed to go where he was really needed. He coolly explained that his experience had taught him that children were abused behind closed doors, often in the best neighborhoods. She looked back at him just as coolly and replied,

"Not here…not in this house! She's a woman of faith!"

He retorted, "Even women of faith are capable of beating their children!"

I escorted him to the door with tears in my eyes, my stomach tied up in a bundle of nerves, and my head pounding from a massive migraine. Michael kept asking if the bad man was coming back for his dad, or his brother, or possibly him. I hugged and kissed him on his forehead and told him not to worry.

In the coming weeks, this same inspector came to question my children at their schools. Phone calls and letters from Child Protective Services arrived almost daily. Every time I heard from them, I became sick to my stomach. I had to communicate with a social worker each and every day during the investigation. It was a horrendous, despicable, and frightening ordeal. Then, after three months of humiliation, stress, and prying investigations, all charges were dropped. No apologies were ever given.

For the longest time afterwards, I would replay the visit from the man in the electric blue Dodge Ram truck with bright silver rims in my head. I knew deep down inside he was only doing his job, but I still stung from the accusations. The memory of it all made me keep questioning our parenting skills, allowing Anthony to go "where the wild things are" every once in a while. Each time I came to the same conclusion. As parents, we were trying our best with what God gave us, but it was simply impossible to be everywhere for everyone all the time. So we needed to forgive him and ourselves. It was essential to our happiness as a family to put this entire experience behind us once and for all. Wallowing in doubt and self- pity wasn't getting us anywhere. We had to rely on the hope that future days would be better.

CHAPTER 16

"The Dreaded Phone Call - One of Many"

I'm So Sorry, Mr. Officer

*J*t had been a couple of nights of interrupted sleep, or no sleep at all. Just a few days before, we had received a court summons taken out by a supposedly close friend of mine, who was suing us for an incident that occurred in our home while she was babysitting our two children, one of whom is disabled. As I tossed and turned, I thought about what else I would have to deal with in the future. You know that saying *my plate is full?* Well my plate is not a plate, but a very large platter!

Unlike his brother Michael, Anthony, Jr. was the little boy we could never get to board the school bus in the morning without causing a problem. His tantrums had become our morning routine. I knew that I loved him beyond words, but what I didn't know was how to help him.

I know that I have mentioned before that I was extremely grateful for his matron and bus driver who were my angels in disguise. These ladies had a combination of patience and compassion rarely seen with such consistency on this earth. The love and acceptance they showered on those children was totally without boundaries. Even though I knew Anthony could not help being the way that he was, I must admit that there were days when I just did not want to be the mother of that kid who could not control himself or behave properly. Whenever those thoughts flashed into my brain, the accompanying guilt would inevitably find its way in as well.

During this time, I had become accustomed to receiving a phone call from the school every day (sometimes twice) about Anthony's inappropriate behaviors at school. It was a few minutes past noon on March 2, 2005 when the phone rang. I had just sat down to fold some laundry. I looked at my caller ID and saw that it was the school. Although I had come to expect these daily calls, my heart began racing with fear, and my mind became anxious. It was the principal from Anthony's school, informing me that my son had had a major meltdown, but that he could not give me details over the phone. In a concerned voice, he instructed me to be there within 15 minutes or they would have to take him by ambulance to be admitted to the hospital. I questioned if Anthony was seriously hurt, but his brief response was that we would talk when I arrived at the school.

In a state of panic, I jumped into my car and took off, fully aware that I only had a few minutes to get to that school before the ambulance would be there to take my baby away. All I kept repeating to myself was to take deep breaths... deep breaths... and I would arrive safely and on time. The drive there felt like forever. I prayed as I drove onto the parkway, not realizing I was driving at least 70 miles an hour. As I passed Exit 24, I saw flashing lights behind my car. All I could think of was getting to Exit 25 where my son was waiting for me.

Ignoring the consequences, I had made up my mind - I was not going to pull over. I watched the police car in my rear view mirror as it closely followed me off the exit and to the front of the school. As I rushed out of my car, the officer approached me and asked why I was speeding and told me to show him my license and registration.

I resolutely answered, "Officer, my son goes to this school. You can do what you have to do, but I'm going into the building right now because my son is not well. This is an emergency!"

As I turned to dash up the stairs, I handed him my wallet and told him to write whatever tickets he felt were necessary. I then promised that I would come out after I saw my son.

My hands were sweaty; I thought my heart was going to come out of my chest as I ran to his classroom. There, I found Anthony lying in a fetal position on the floor in a corner of the room. He had trashed the entire classroom, flipping over the desks, ripping school work off the walls, and finally passing out from the intensity of his rage. He had become so out of control that he had to be isolated away from the other students while the staff monitored his actions through the door. I picked him up off the floor and saw that his pants were soiled. He was sleeping peacefully. Could this be the same child that had so violently wrecked his classroom? I walked down the hallway carrying him in my arms like a baby, and stepped out through the front door.

The officer was waiting by my car; he looked at my face and didn't say a word. I put Anthony in his booster seat and went over to the officer.

In a sympathetic voice, he observed, "You look like you're having a very difficult day."

I began to cry and hyperventilate. "Please quickly write up my tickets so I can leave!"

"My nephew is autistic. I knew what type of school it was when I pulled up in front of it. Look, you have a clean driving record so I'll let you off with a verbal warning. But drive carefully so you can bring you child home safely."

I was very fortunate that the officer was understanding and decent. This terrible day could have ended up very differently if had decided to place me in handcuffs for not pulling over. I could have very well been arrested for ignoring his directions. Even worse, my reckless driving may have injured not only myself, but others. This was a blessing in disguise, confirming my belief in the existence of guardian angels that unexpectedly appear to save us from ourselves.

As I tried to find out what was at the bottom of Anthony's outburst, I remembered that his neurologist had put him on the ADHD medication Adderall, which had been giving him bad headaches that were making him very irritable. Since this medication had received some negative reviews, I was reluctant about putting him on it. Unfortunately I did not listen to my inner voice and trusted the neurologist instead. This was a major life lesson: doctors and specialists were not always right!

As parents and guardians, we must remind doctors of the fact that we are with our children all day, every day. Therefore, we know them better than anyone else. The fact is that most physicians and specialists come in contact with our children for less than an hour every month or every three months, yet they believe they know what's best for them. From my perspective, this does not make sense. One of the most important roles we have as parents is to inform the professionals about our children to help them see the full picture. Sometimes, we will need to strongly express our disagreement with the doctor, no matter how renowned he or she is, and in doing so, you will discover that your opinion will not only be heard, but valued.

CHAPTER 17

"Where do I Belong?"

Anthony, Jr Is Permanently Removed From Kindergarten

*I*t is August 12, 2003, a day I was not looking forward to: my district meeting for Anthony Jr.'s transition from pre-school to kindergarten. At the time, he was labeled "Other Health Impaired." Anthony's godmother, an experienced special education teacher, decided to accompany me to this meeting because my emotions were on overdrive. At the meeting, it was decided that he would be placed in another elementary school that housed a self-contained kindergarten.

His kindergarten teacher there had a heart of gold and was especially dedicated to my son. As a skilled, compassionate teacher, she knew that his transition into kindergarten was going to be challenging. He was having trouble recognizing letters and numbers, struggling to pay attention, having mild seizures, and battling with himself and others to fit into his new surroundings. She would take time to sit with him every day in order to help and observe him. It was easy to see that a special relationship was developing between them. However, the administrative staff was not experienced or qualified enough to even have a child like Anthony in the building. I received one phone call after the next, which only heightened my sense of uneasiness with the situation.

I just had this intense, recurring feeling that they did not want my son in that school. The principal appeared to have a heart made of stone. For example, on one occasion my son called him a liar. Anthony's reason for doing so was that he had been provoked by the principal's dishonesty, but as a punishment, Anthony was sent straight to the principal's office. I later discovered that his explanation was not that far off from the truth. I saw how my son was trying to adapt and do what was expected of him. Unfortunately his best efforts failed. I became so frustrated and upset that it broke my heart (not the first or the last of many such heartbreaks...)

I began to understand why he fought so hard not to get on the "big boy" bus in the morning. Every day it was a different story. One day, in order to escape, he ran around the corner, past my neighbor's home. I had no choice but to let the bus leave without him because

Anthony was nowhere in sight. He could run like the wind; it made him feel both free and in control at the same time. My neighbor reacted without hesitation, jumping into his car to begin searching for my son. Thank God for my neighbors! He found him several blocks away. After placing him safely in the car, he asked what was wrong.

Anthony told him, "I don't belong in that school."

He came home in tears. I decided it would be best if he stayed home, considering the difficult morning. I also feared what would happen at school that day.

In February 2004, I felt that it was important to discuss the situation privately with my district's special education director. She listened to me carefully and decided that Anthony should have a psychiatric evaluation. She then recommended a pediatric psychiatrist with 31 years of experience in providing specialized services for children with developmental disorders. I felt very fortunate to have such a patient, distinguished and well qualified doctor assess my son. Without this professional's input, I would never have been able to navigate this *Alice-in-Wonderland-like* system known as "special- ed" so skillfully all these years.

As time went by, I realized that Anthony's days at that school had to come to an end. It just wasn't working out for anyone. Every day presented us with new difficulties, and it became intolerable for me as a mother, never knowing what new horror would occur. We made it all the way through to spring; April 1st would be his final day. Yet even so, I received a phone call early that morning, advising me to pick him up immediately. It was absolutely clear that he was no longer welcome there. It was time to start down a new path.

His teacher had tried her best to keep him in her class, but the administration had different ideas altogether. I will always remember that she had had his best interests at heart and for that, she will always have a special place in my heart. He was out of school 71 days that year, not a good situation for any child.

After all the evaluations, it was decided that the best place for him in the coming September would be at the local school for special needs children. I kept my fingers crossed, prayed a lot, and hoped that this choice would work for him and our family. Only time would tell.

CHAPTER 18

"Ignorance is Bliss"

The Costco Fiasco

*I*t was a typically hot day in the summer that Anthony, Jr. was five years old and Michael was three. My husband suggested a trip to Costco for some bulk shopping and a change of scene. As a mother of young children, I knew that such a venture could go either way, but I also realized that my husband wanted to get out of the house to lose himself among the tools and man cave accessories. For my part, I would have preferred going to the dentist for a tooth extraction rather than trekking over to Costco with my two small children on a blistering Saturday, when it is usually jam-packed with carts pushed by rude shoppers with tunnel vision.

At this stage in our lives, my husband still wanted to believe that we were a typical family of four going on a shopping run. However, I could have easily predicted from recent experiences that this trip was not a good idea. Against my better judgment though, my husband was able to convince me that we needed to stock up for the summer barbeque season with frozen meats, drinks, snacks, condiments, etc... I gave in, simply because it was too hot to argue, and because maybe, just maybe, I was being too cautious.

So, we packed the children in the car with some goldfish snacks and boxed drinks. We started singing *How Much is That Doggie in the Window?* They both loved that song so we sang it over and over again until before we knew it, we had arrived. My husband went to grab a cart, while I unbuckled the boys from their seats. I instantly noticed that Anthony, Jr.'s eyes were glazed over and he appeared listless, but I decided to ignore these tell-tale signs, telling myself that once he was in the store, he would be just fine.

Upon entering the store, we headed for the meat section to pick up some chicken cutlets, steaks, hamburgers, and hot dogs. Immediately afterwards, we went to the breakfast aisle where I searched for Cheerios among what seemed like hundreds of cereal boxes piled from ceiling to floor. All of a sudden, Anthony, Jr. started to grow restless and began fidgeting and fussing like most children his age, but then his behavior progressed into a major meltdown, which is more dramatic than a childish temper tantrum. An older couple walked by and I could see that the woman was annoyed with my son's uncontrollable outburst. Every parent knows the repercussions of such a public display by a child: the shoppers staring with disapproval, coupled with your own anxiety and embarrassment, not to mention that feeling of utter helplessness

My husband saw that Michael was also getting nervous, so he picked him up to comfort him. I followed his example by taking Anthony, Jr. into my arms, and sat us down together on a huge crate so I could rub his back and calm him down. Remember that older couple?

As they passed us by, the woman snidely said, "If he was my kid, I'd give him a beating!"

My husband knew what was coming. He put Michael in the wagon and I handed him Anthony, Jr.

I glared back at her and retorted, "Thank God he's not your son! My son has a disability. So what's your excuse?"

The man appeared to be mortified by his wife's actions.

Of course at this point I really wanted to go home and forget about how ignorance is bliss. Once I had confirmed that Anthony, Jr. had calmed down, I agreed to continue shopping for our supplies. I understood now that my older son would get very overwhelmed in certain places because of his processing delays. Next, he would feel frustrated by not being able to understand his own emotions, and then become further anguished at not being able to clearly communicate his distress with us. (Hell, I get overwhelmed in certain places!)

I heard Anthony sigh wistfully, "Mommy, my stomach is telling me I'm hungry."

So that was why he was crying! That stranger wanted me to beat my child because she lacked the imagination to see that he was hungry, had trouble expressing it, and was developmentally delayed. I hoped that the Costco Granny was not a real grandmother because God help her grandchildren if they ever misbehaved!

We took the boys to the concession stand where we sat and fed the boys. As I went for a refill of my fountain drink, I saw Costco Granny's husband. He wanted to apologize for her. I politely thanked him for his decency, but told him to advise his wife that she should keep her thoughts to herself because you can never know the circumstances surrounding a situation.

My advice to everyone reading this is that when you see someone struggling with a child - any child - anywhere, simply ask if you can help in any way. Why do you need to judge? Offer your assistance instead of your opinion. At this point in time, our society should be well aware of the heartbreak of a parent that has a child with special needs. You would be amazed at what that parent's reaction would be to the kindness you extended, instead of the usual stares and derision she has sadly come to expect.

After this long, distressful day, the boys were placed in bed. I received a phone call from my friend Laura, my neighbor who lives down the block. She wanted to know if I would like to hang out and watch a movie. She is my "girly" girlfriend, the one who always knows how bargain shopping and picking out great accessories would perk up her pal when she was having a very bad day. She was that person for me, the one whose door was always open for a cup of coffee, a quick lunch, or a heart-to-heart chat. (On top of everything, she was also a very good listener!)

Well, tonight I really needed to have some adult conversation with my friend, while eating some sweet-and-salty snacks and watching "The Notebook." (By the way, it's a great chick-flick.) She asked how my day had gone, and I started venting about our Costco run, knowing that Laura would be the voice of enlightenment.

She came through as usual, telling me, "People like that need your prayers, not your anger. You should feel sorry for them because they don't know any better. Do they?"

I understood that I needed to stop being resentful and start heeding my girlfriend's advice. Her advice made me realize that people are only human and usually find it difficult to understand the problems that others face on a daily basis.

That night I prayed for Costco Granny, her husband, and others like them. I prayed that, for the sake of my son and his fellow travelers, humanity's heart would be filled with love, empathy and compassion. I asked God to give them the gift of insight to truly see what was in front of them without passing judgment. Amen.

CHAPTER 19

"Community Nursery School"

All by Myself

*J*n September of 2001, Anthony, Jr. had just entered nursery school. I will never forget his first day of school. My stomach was sick with the fear of knowing how difficult the separation was going to be for both of us, even though it was only for a few hours in the afternoon, three days a week.

His two nursery school teachers were quick to notice that Anthony, Jr. had developmental delays. I wanted to believe his slow progress was caused by his epilepsy, but deep down I knew it was more than that. As a young scared mother, I was struck by their commitment as well as by their support. A few years later, when Michael attended the school, one of these same teachers actually potty trained him, a milestone that I thought was never going to happen. Anthony was potty trained at twenty months, but Michael just didn't want to get out of those diapers! This dedicated teacher took on that task like a proud mama and succeeded.

While Anthony had some good days, there were some days that were not so good and on those days, I received phone calls. He was frustrated with himself because he had a hard time socializing with children his age. Yet, despite the uphill battle, his two teachers continued working with him.

On the days I was called into the school, I would find Anthony in the director's office. He was sent there whenever he needed a break from the classroom, and she would place him on her lap and play games with him. She would sing with him, and give him coloring books, action figures and puzzles for amusement. She was the sweetest, most loving, and compassionate person that I met at the beginning of Anthony's school days. She always knew what he truly wanted, whether it was a snack, a drink, a hug, a song, or just a bit of one-on-one quality time. She delivered just that. He loved being in her office with her, all by himself.

Although I was confused and frustrated with Anthony's apparent discomfort inside the classroom, I felt quite comfortable with his placement at that school. His safety was never a concern for me; it was his inability to make friends, or to recognize letters and numbers that concerned me. No matter how many flash cards and learning games I tried out with him, Anthony just couldn't remember or retain what we had just gone over a few minutes earlier. All that practice only heightened my concerns and fears. *What was wrong with my son???*

At the age of two, Anthony would play and socialize at *Tots on Track*, but when I left him alone in the play area with the other children, he would cry and hold his breath until he was blue. This behavior began at a *Mommy and Me* session when the children separated from their parents to play with their peers. Moreover, Anthony had a lot of difficulty sitting still, playing with others, and following rules. So, from the very beginning, it was obvious that he was not developing at the same pace as the other children his age.

To look at him, you would never be able to see that anything could possibly be "wrong" or "abnormal." Yet, I knew that something was not right when I saw how he struggled with simple tasks that came so easily for other children. Those were the dark days, the days of self-doubt, self-pity, and rage.

At the same time, my mom had been diagnosed with uterine cancer and needed a full hysterectomy. The circumstances surrounding her diagnosis were indeed miraculous. Thank God she came through unscathed because I am not quite sure what I would do without her. She is the matriarch and a great support to my children and family. It wasn't always that way, but it is now. I am forever grateful for her.

CHAPTER 20

"Am I Going to Die?"

My Diagnosis with Graves' Disease

*A*fter Michael's birth in June of 2001, I felt my body was not healthy. My hands were always shaking and my hair was falling out. I was deeply depressed and sometimes unable to catch my breath. My skin was constantly burning, my weight loss was ongoing, and my bowels were loose. These symptoms continued for months. I knew something had to be wrong, but I ignored my instincts.

The truth was that my worries over my son Anthony not only clouded my judgment, but also intensified my fears. I really didn't want to know what was wrong with me; I just hoped everything would get better on its own. I finally heeded the advice of close friends who had been urging me to take some kind of action and went to see my primary care physician. His diagnosis was "anxiety due to the September 11th attacks." I tried to explain that what I was feeling was more than just anxiety. He prescribed Buspar, which I never took. I never realized that things could go from bad to worse in an instant.

Three months passed with no significant improvement. One morning, I went to the gym for my usual workout… the last thing I remembered was cycling with five minutes to go. In a nano-second, my heart began racing and I blacked out. Needless to say, that episode scared me into reality. If something were to happen to me, who would raise my children and advocate for them?

I went straight to the doctor's office for an emergency appointment. It was time for a second opinion. I followed my intuition and requested a blood test for autoimmune disease. The blood results revealed that I had something called "Graves' Disease," an autoimmune disorder that affects the thyroid. I had a large goiter, with high levels of thyroid hormone that were attacking my heart and vital organs. I learned that Graves' disease would cause the body to produce antibodies to the receptor for thyroid-stimulating hormone (TSH).

I was referred to an endocrinologist who specialized in glands and diseases of the glands. He ran more tests and explained that doctors don't like to remove the thyroid unless it was absolutely necessary. He prescribed Propranolol, which is a beta blocker that blocks the effects of hormones on the body and Methimazole (or Tapazole), an anti-thyroid medication. Seemingly endless months of uncertainty, irritability, anxiety and frustration followed this diagnosis. Of course, I wanted to get better yesterday, but I knew my recovery would most likely be a much longer process than I wanted it to be.

In fact, I was on medication for approximately four years until I was given a radioactive iodine treatment in February 2005. With this therapy, you take radioactive iodine (or radioiodine) by mouth. The thyroid needs iodine to produce hormones, so it consumes the radioiodine, which then destroys the overactive thyroid cells over time. The hoped-for outcome was that my thyroid gland would slowly begin to shrink, and the symptoms to gradually decrease within several weeks to several months.

Unfortunately, I needed two doses of radioactive iodine because in my case, one dose was not enough (*naturally!*). Torture me, why don't you? What made matters worse was that I needed to stay at my parents' home in their basement because I could not be near my children for at least three days due to the radioactive iodine.

I decided since I was marooned there, I might as well make good use of my time. I asked my mom to put highlights in my hair, which she had done before on many occasions. However, this time, she left the highlights in for so long that I turned into a platinum blonde. (I have jet black hair.) All I wanted was a few highlights to cover the grey! When I looked in the mirror, I was traumatized. My mother didn't know what to say. Her first response was,

"Oh my God!"

She followed with, "Don't worry-hair grows."

After that, who needed to look in the mirror? Until then, I thought my hairstylist could correct my mother's handiwork. Not really! Whenever anyone would see me, their first questions were all about my hair, not my health. I could not conceive what they were thinking. Some of them even thought it was a side effect of the radioactive iodine. LOL!

After that second dose of radioactive iodine and follow-up thyroid medications, my levels gradually became close to normal. Thyroid disease is more serious than it sounds since the thyroid controls your body temperature, weight, thinking, nervous system and other organs. In short, if your thyroid is off, everything else is off too.

A word to the wise: Don't ignore signs when your body is trying to tell you something is wrong. I was playing chess with Death and he was winning. My friends and family pushed me to take care of myself. Without them, I probably wouldn't be here.

CHAPTER 21

"My Eventful Trip to Target"

The Arrival of Michael

$\mathcal{J}$t was June 2001 and I had two weeks of waiting until our second son was to be born. Anyone who has been pregnant knows that towards the end of your last trimester, you just want the baby out! To make matters worse, it was the beginning of those hot summer days and I was waddling around, tired and swollen. My condition, however, did not stop me from shopping with my mom at Target for a few extra baby supplies.

We arrived at Target in the late afternoon because it was just too stifling earlier in the day to do much of anything. As we walked towards the store, I told my mom that I was feeling a lot of pressure below…and then unwisely pushed the thought out of my head.

I had my list of various baby needs and slowly hobbled about the store picking up various items (t-shirts, diapers, bibs, burping cloths, pajamas, etc…). As I checked off the last few items on my list, I turned to look at my shopping cart and it was gone. I looked around in disbelief that someone had taken my wagon. So I started to roam the aisles to search for it, but to no avail; my cart filled with my precious baby items was nowhere to be found. I was fit to be tied! After all, I was nine months pregnant, and in no condition to be wandering around a store that I had just purposefully made my way around already!

Then suddenly, to make matters even worse, I felt a tingling wet sensation. This was strange, but in my present mood, I thought nothing of it. My mom was telling me to relax, but stubborn creature that I am, I continued on my mission. We went to security to ask them to page customers to see if anyone had "mistakenly" taken a wagon with baby items. However, no sooner was the announcement made, that my water broke! Yep, that was the wet tingling sensation. My mom's sound advice was to leave the items and come back for them later.

I argued with her, sarcastically asking, "When? When the baby is born? After all this? No! I don't think so!"

At that point, my wagon was returned by a customer who hadn't realized her mistake. I was extremely impatient and hormonal. All I kept thinking was about how the customer had a wagon full of baby items. How could she not notice? Soon after, we paid for all the baby items and went to my parents' home.

At 11:31PM that night, Michael came into the world via C-section… two weeks earlier than anticipated. My second prince had come into the world. Just when I thought my heart wasn't big enough to love another child unconditionally, I was proven wrong.

CHAPTER 22

"It's Time!"

The Arrival of Anthony, Jr

*N*ine months had passed and I was consumed with the worry and fear of not only becoming a new parent, but also with thoughts of how this baby would affect our fledgling marriage. We had conceived the child on the first night of our honeymoon and so were still considered newlyweds. As most newly married couples, we were trying to become accustomed to living together under the same roof, and now we also needed to adjust to parenthood – both in such a short period of time!

It was October 15, 1998... I remember very vividly standing in my kitchen barefoot and pregnant, wondering if this would be the day for the arrival of our son. I was barefoot because even my most lived-in shoes no longer fit comfortably on my swollen feet. My belly was so extended that I could no longer see those swollen feet or bend down to put closed shoes on. UGH!

All I kept thinking was *"Let today be the day!"*

I hadn't really slept the night before because it was so difficult to get comfortable, and most of the time I suffered with acid reflux. Throughout my pregnancy I suffered with morning sickness. In reality, for me it was morning, noon, and night sickness. My husband would constantly find me in the bathroom with my head in the bowl. In retrospect, I don't really think my husband had a clue as to what I was going through since my hormones were fluctuating and my body was constantly changing. No matter how many books you read, nothing can ever prepare you for any of this.

As I think back on that beautiful October day, I remember folding laundry in my kitchen, feeling quite uncomfortable due to the pressure inflicted on my spine while standing. At 5PM, a pain so indescribably sharp and intense took hold of my body. I thought to myself that this had to be the anxiously anticipated beginning of the so-called contractions! I called my husband at work to let him know my contractions had started. He asked if I was OK, and then told me in a very gentle voice that he loved me and we would soon be parents.

He arrived from work that evening around 7:15pm and kissed me and my belly. We decided to go to the diner that was within walking distance so he could eat. Even though my discomfort was growing, I decided to eat toast with a cup of chicken noodle soup.

We arrived at the hospital around 8:45pm and I was admitted to the obstetrics floor. The nurse gave me a hospital gown and asked that I walk around the hospital to help induce labor. Unfortunately, after walking an hour with ever increasing pain, there was no progress. After what seemed like forever, they finally took us into the family birthing room. My mom asked to stay with us and I was very pleased that she did.

My doctor broke my water and my son defecated inside of me. This is known as Meconium Aspiration. Approximately 15 minutes later, I vomited all over the doctor's fashionable Armani shoes. (I guess that's why they tell you not to eat before giving birth, but really - what was he thinking by wearing such expensive shoes in that room in the first place???) I continued to push and push for many hours with no significant progress. My husband was so exhausted from working all day and being with me through these pain-filled hours of labor, so I was fortunate to have my mom in the birthing room with me.

At one point, I told her something was very wrong. I knew my baby was stuck because I could feel him lodged behind my hips. She immediately understood the danger and told the doctor that if he didn't take the baby from me *right now*, she would either lose me, her grandson, or both of us.

The specialist agreed my mother's instructions: my son was not to be born naturally, but by C-section because I had a genetic disorder that prevented my hips from expanding while giving birth. The delivery room was prepped and I gave birth on October 16th at approximately 6:54am to Anthony, Jr. My husband cried as he held his son for the first time. As they put him on my chest, I experienced the unique sensation of being a mother. All the agony, fear, and anxiety were forgotten. My entire family was given the news in the waiting area and my mom could finally breathe easily.

The next day my parents saw their grandson for the first time. I noticed that my mother's face was ashen, but in the fog of optimism that always surrounds a new baby, I decided it was due to her lack of sleep. Anthony, Jr. was sleeping in the hospital bassinette so we waited patiently for his feeding time. My dad had gone to the cafeteria for some coffee and rolls.

Finally my prince awakened and I handed him over to my mom. As she cradled her grandson in her arms for the first time, she collapsed onto my bed. I forced myself to ignore my initial shock and rang the buzzer for the nurses' desk. As soon as a nurse arrived, I screamed that something was wrong with my mom. She was quickly placed in a wheelchair and taken to the emergency room for tests.

I was a brand new mom and now my mom was in intensive care a few floors below me. I just could not seem to wrap my head around any of it. It was simply incredible. Was this really happening? I wanted desperately to see her, but was prevented from doing so because she had had a nuclear medical test. Since this quarantine was just a precautionary measure, the next day I decided to take matters into my own hands.

Despite the warnings and my being in recovery for my C-section, I slowly walked over to the next wing and took the elevator down. As I was congratulating myself on my gutsy initiative, the fire alarm sounded, the elevator stopped in between floors, and the water sprinklers went off. Now what? This was what I got for not obeying the rules! About 20 minutes later, the sprinklers stopped and the elevator inched its way down to the lobby. Great... I was soaking wet in my silky green pajamas! I still had to find out if my mom was fine in the middle of all of this chaos, and then return to the maternity ward in time to feed my son.

I eventually made my way back to maternity, only to be scolded by the head nurse for my misdeeds. I also discovered that my mom had indeed had a heart attack due to both the excitement and lack of sleep over the birth of her grandson. I was actually released a day before my mom. All turned out alright for everyone all those years ago. Yet, I should have known from the very beginning that the intensity of my son's entry into the world would be a foreshadowing of the drama to follow!

TRUE DIRECTIONS

An affiliate of Tarcher Books

OUR MISSION

Tarcher's mission has always been to publish books
that contain great ideas. Why? Because:

GREAT LIVES BEGIN WITH GREAT IDEAS

At Tarcher, we recognize that many talented authors, speakers,
educators, and thought-leaders share this mission and deserve to be
published – many more than Tarcher can reasonably publish ourselves.
True Directions is ideal for authors and books that increase awareness,
raise consciousness, and inspire others to live their ideals and passions.

Like Tarcher, True Directions books are designed to do three things:
inspire, inform, and motivate.

Thus, True Directions is an ideal way for these important voices
to bring their messages of hope, healing, and help to the world.

Every book published by True Directions– whether it is non-
fiction, memoir, novel, poetry or children's book – continues
Tarcher's mission to publish works that bring positive change
in the world. We invite you to join our mission.

For more information, see the True Directions website:
www.iUniverse.com/TrueDirections/SignUp

Be a part of Tarcher's community to bring positive change in this world!
See exclusive author videos, discover new and exciting books, learn about
upcoming events, connect with author blogs and websites, and more!
www.tarcherbooks.com

TRUE DIRECTIONS
AN AFFILIATE OF TARCHER BOOKS